Solo Acoustic Musician™

A Practical How-To Guide

Michael Nichols

Printed in the United States of America

ISBN: 978-1-953910-68-4 (paperback)
ISBN: 978-1-953910-70-7 (ebook)

Canoe Tree
Press

4697 Main Street
Manchester Center, VT 05255

Canoe Tree Press is a division of DartFrog Books.

TABLE OF CONTENTS

 # INTRODUCTION

It was early spring in 1990 and I had just turned fourteen. I asked a close friend who was sixteen and already driving if he would take me to a bar so I could ask for a gig. I had a conversation with the owner and I walked out of that bar with a big smile on my face, having booked the first paying gig of my life!

Getting that first gig on my calendar gave me a rush of confidence, and before I had even played, I had lined up three more places to play. I was hooked, and I knew what I wanted to do with my life. It did not take long before I was performing every Friday and Saturday night at bars and restaurants all over town. That was thirty years ago, and I have learned a lot along the way.

I consider this book to be a stripped-down, uncomplicated version of a fairly complex adventure into the world of being a Solo Acoustic Musician, or SAM, based on my unique personal perspective and experiences. When there were no rules to follow or classes to take, I set out to create my own path, and now I am sharing what I've learned with you. From forming a song list to booking a date to performing, I had to learn (sometimes repeatedly) from my many failures and also my successes.

This book provides career advice for anyone, novice or professional, who wants to earn money as a working SAM.

It includes guidance on performing in bars and restaurants, planning ahead for all kinds of situations, and being prepared for them. Most of this book seems to be common sense to me. But I know sometimes we all need a third-party perspective to help us move forward and grow into a better version of ourselves. Every SAM explores this lifestyle in their own way.

One thing that's interesting to me about our particular profession is that we can play other people's songs and make a living. You cannot do the same thing in most other professions. You would not expect to see someone author a "cover book." By the same token, you cannot make a living telling someone else's jokes. A "cover comedian" is a nonexistent thing. If you tell someone else's jokes for money, you will probably be ostracized by the comedy community. It is just not acceptable in their world.

One obvious goal of this book is to help younger up-and-coming Solo Acoustic Musicians avoid some of the mistakes that I made when I was starting out. Also, I believe that kids whose parents are taking an active interest in helping them succeed at becoming full-time Solo Acoustic Musicians will probably find some valuable tips in this book, too.

When you are a SAM, you are on your own. Yes, you can network with other musicians, and yes, you have your family and friends for support, but ultimately you are on your own. You can make a living, play music, and have a productive life all at the same time. There has never been a better time to be a SAM!

If you are in a band then you can go on stage with a few other people, which is an upside... but the downside is that the bars and restaurants that will book you will pay less. It doesn't really make any sense that they will pay $150-300 for a solo artist and then only pay $300-500 for a full band;

it is horrible math. But for a SAM it doesn't matter. I make more money and also avoid all the pitfalls of trying to book a five-piece band. I only have one schedule and calendar to look after. I pay my bills on time and I use my skills to take a vacation each year.

There are lots of schools of thought on how to do this as an occupation, but these are my ideas and experiences. I really love what I do for a living, but don't get me wrong, everything in life has its ups and downs. This profession is no different. There will be trying times and times of absolute positivity. To make a career or lifestyle out of being a SAM, you will be tested.

In order to stay on top of your game and flourish for many years, you will need to have a thick skin and deal with constant criticism. For whatever reason, people complain way more than they show appreciation. So laugh it off and don't let it stop you from pursuing your dreams of making a living playing music.

I started out with lofty goals of getting a record deal and becoming an iconic star of my generation. To be clear, every twelve-year-old who picks up a guitar probably has the same intentions. I never gave up hope or settled on a profession I didn't want to do, but I did find a way to make a living and sustain a lifestyle that fulfills my desires to make people smile. I truly enjoy playing and singing songs for people. It has been what I have done my whole life, and although there are good days and bad days, it has been the one constant in my life. People, places, and things come and go, but who I am and what I am remains a constant.

I don't feel any regret in becoming who I am. I became a SAM and I have come to understand that I am a valuable part of my community. I have made friends, made a living, and dealt with many different situations, all of which have made me a better person and a better musician. I don't sit in a cubicle at an office, I don't report to a boss, I'm not cutting grass on a golf course or lifting heavy boxes in a warehouse. I can move to any city that I want to and I can dictate my own life. I have skills that allow me to travel the world and see things that other people save up for.

I wish I'd had a book like this to read when I was starting out. I hope that you will find the following information helpful on your journey. Have fun, stay the course, and enjoy your life as a fellow Solo Acoustic Musician.

 # ALWAYS BE ON TIME

---

*"You always gotta be on time,
an hour ahead of everything.
You always gotta be prepared."*
—Beanie Sigel

I think the importance of always being on time was instilled in me when I was a kid. It was always part of the program with my parents, teachers, and other influential adults in my life. As an adult, I have to admit that everything they were telling me about punctuality was true. I believe it is an important part of being a professional and taking my gigs seriously. Promptness is essential to many important achievements in life and starting out my gigs by running late is not in my playbook. Being on time can also be a measure of someone's sincerity and commitment to a project or a gig with you, so keep that in mind if you book yourself on shared gigs with other musicians. A shared gig can be one where each SAM takes a turn to play a set.

My usual practice is to be on the site of the gig one hour before my starting time, especially if it is the first time I am playing a new location. Over the years, several places have actually called me when it was ten after the hour that I would usually arrive, wondering where I was. I have answered my cell phone only a few blocks away to explain to them that the traffic and weather had delayed my arrival. It was nice to know that they had taken notice of the fact that I was punctual; that made me feel like I was doing the right thing simply by always being on time. I have been known to tell my friends and other musicians that I would rather be early than run late and then arrive in a stressful state after trying to get there. Consistency is a big word in business, so if you can make arriving on time an important part of your process, people will notice your work ethic.

Have you ever been on your way to a gig and run into heavy traffic due to an accident, or the holiday traffic associated with seasonal tourists? In reality, I only need about ten to fifteen minutes to set up all of my gear. But situationally, I may have to accommodate my schedule due to traffic, weather, parking situations, and load-in distances. (For example, you might have to park in a parking garage down the street and walk for five to ten minutes to get to the venue. Or you might have to bring your equipment from the parking garage to the tenth floor of a big hotel by elevator.) These things can add up to set me back and cause me to arrive on the job site with minimal time to set up. It is just a great reason to always leave the house a little early. I have also noticed that it consistently takes a lot longer to get to the gig than to get home afterward. This is most likely because of traffic density due to the time of day. There are a lot fewer cars on the road coming home late at night.

I keep things in my van to occupy my time if I am too early. In case I anticipate extra traffic due to the Fourth of July or some other holiday or event, then happen to arrive very early because it doesn't materialize, I bring a book to read. I also bring my clipboard and calendar with me, to make notes and do work while I am waiting. I might send out some texts or emails from my phone in that spare time. Sometimes I am able to book some gigs right there in my van while I am passing the time before I can load-in and set up.

Depending on the location of the gig, this can also be a good time to walk around and look for another place to play. Sometimes, though, I just enjoy the location. For example, I play a steady Sunday evening gig on the beach at sunset in Clearwater Beach, Florida, and the traffic on the bridge leading there can really vary. I give myself plenty of time and often get there really early. But finding parking can be an issue. So if I am really early, I can get a snack at the place I play and hang out on the beach until it's time to set up. Clearwater Beach is a busy beach town, and in the past I have walked around when I was early and found new places to play. It just depends on my mood and what I feel like doing with that spare time. I will say this, I would rather be early than be stuck on the bridge for an hour, and then have to drive around looking for parking. That really would be a very stressful situation to have to endure.

There have been times when I am early to my destination and a festival or event is right down the street from my gig. I will take a walk to see the live bands and check out the vendors. I have made some new musician friends this way. I have also met some musicians who I had heard of, but never actually met in person, even though we had both been playing some of the same places for years. Many of us are already friends on Facebook, though, and so it is nice to have a random encounter with them in person.

When I book a gig with a venue owner or manager, we are basically entering into a contractual agreement with set parameters. They are going to pay me to provide a service and to play for a certain amount of time, and that gig has both a start time and an end time. This is just another reason why it is important to always be on time. It is also important to fulfill the contract by not stopping early. I have seen owners point to their watch or the clock on the wall when a musician stops playing early. I am talking about less than five minutes before the agreed finish time, which doesn't seem like that much, but it is a business arrangement and some owners are not laid back about a performer finishing early on a gig.

A manager once confided in me about another Solo Acoustic Musician who was constantly showing up about fifteen minutes after they were supposed to begin playing. She said she really liked the musician and thought he was very talented, but after the third and fourth time he showed up late, she quit booking him. I can understand her position, and I know she must appreciate the fact that I am always on time. It's just another example of how people who are paying you are making mental notes about how you operate. Even when I don't notice it, I have to remember that they are paying attention to what I am doing on the gig.

I knew a band once that actually broke up fighting over being on time. Surprisingly, the main culprit was the drummer, which I found ironic because the drummer is in charge of the time. He constantly arrived at gigs at the time the band was supposed to start playing. I opened up for them once and the whole band's backline (the backline will usually consist of a drum set, amps for the guitars, bass, and keyboards, and microphones and direct boxes, and is usually provided by the host band, the event organizer, or the soundman who also provides the P.A. for a concert) was set up before I started my set, except for the drums. When I was done with my one-hour set and it was time for them to kick off their show, their drummer was literally just pulling his truck up to the curb in front of the building. I could feel the tension and embarrassment through the other guys' faces and body language. I am sure they were extremely stressed out, and that can't be a fun way to start your show, feeling like that. Over time it created great dissension amongst the band members, and ultimately was the catalyst for their demise.

It is hard enough to keep a band together without extra problems like these. Do you see how important it can be to be on time? I am not saying that there aren't any extenuating circumstances, because things do happen, but when a pattern of lateness develops, it will cause problems for you.

In the spring of 2019 I left my house early for a gig in Apollo Beach, which is a town on the east side of Tampa, a little more than an hour from me. I wanted to arrive at six PM, so I chose to leave at four-thirty. I thought this would give me plenty of time to get there and not be in a hurry or fall behind. Boy, was I wrong.

I encountered heavy traffic on the 275 to I4 highway interchange. This was a part of the trip I was very used to. But once I was on 275, traffic slowed to a crawl for an accident and everyone had to be funneled down into one lane. This took a while, and I was aware that I was starting to fall behind schedule.

The flow of cars finally picked back up and as I merged onto I4 I moved into the left lane to take the Selmon Expressway. I decided to get off at an exit I had never used before, because I knew the traffic on I75 at this hour would be bad and backed up at the exit I wanted to take. I drove onto Route 41 and headed south. That was when I encountered a construction zone and was once again directed to merge into a single lane.

After getting through the construction zone, I felt like I was making up time and finally moving steadily down the road. That is, until the railroad track signs lit up and the crossbars came down. I actually laughed out loud.

I was at the front of the line of cars and would be the first to go after the train had gone through. I decided to time this event. At the point where I could see the train coming to an end, it stopped. It paused. And then it started to back up! The train did this a few times. I am guessing that they were adding cars to the end. Finally, after twelve and a half minutes, the train moved on. I arrived at my gig at 6:16 PM, after a one-hour-and-forty-six-minute drive.

I gave myself a buffer by leaving early, and arrived later than I wanted to, but I started on time. The gig went great. I made lots of tips. I drove home safely and it only took me forty-five minutes to get back.

To recap: It is very important to always be on time. I will not stop making it one of my priorities when it comes to my gigs or my lifestyle. As a Solo Acoustic Musician, I hope you choose to carry the torch and always be on time.

 **SONG LIST**

---

*"The reason I stop playing songs is usually
because I get sick of them, and then they find
themselves back into the set list at some point."*
—Ben Folds

Having enough songs to play for a three or four hour gig (with breaks) is the starting point. While we all want to play songs we like, we will encounter many requests for songs that we don't like, or don't know how to play. Building a list that offers hundreds of songs to choose from will help alleviate some of the stress that comes with trying to please complete strangers with our song choices.

I always keep a pen and a piece of paper in my pocket to jot down request ideas from audience members. When I get home, I look up the songs on YouTube, and if I can get into it, I will learn a version of a song. Some of my favorite songs that I play now came to be in my list because of a suggestion or request from a complete stranger at a gig. They usually say something like, "You sound like so-and-so; you should play this song, because I think you would sing that person's voice well." I am constantly learning new songs that I want to try out to keep it fresh for myself as well.

I try to learn chord charts, riffs, licks, and songs in many styles. In a way it's kind of like MMA. MMA is short for mixed martial arts, where an individual learns several disciplines or styles of martial arts, in order to be able to compete against a broad range of opponents. The combination of different styles of music and becoming versatile opens up more doors for me. If I were to only play blues, I would be limited in the number and type of venues I could play. The same goes for any other genre. I choose to be diverse and learn songs in many different styles. I believe it helps me in my pursuit of keeping my calendar full. If I am at a golf course restaurant, a dive bar, a tiki bar, a fancy restaurant, an airport, a private party, or a corporate event, I believe I can adapt to the clientele or audience and provide a wide range of songs.

I personally play in several genres and my answer to the question, "What do you play?" is, "I play rock, reggae, blues, and country cover songs."

Physically typing up a song list is a good idea for a couple of reasons. I can use my song list as part of my sales pitch to clients. I can also share my song list with agents who will use it in their pitches to get me gigs. I used to print up my song list and include it in my mailers. Nowadays, I just keep a file on my computer and email it when someone asks me for it. I like to think potential clients are impressed when I send out a list with hundreds of songs on it.

Another reason for typing up my song list is to track my progress with learning and adding new songs. I try to update my list every few months. It helps to keep me current with what I am doing, so that I can share the latest version of my song list. I always have songs being processed and added to my book to keep it fresh for myself on my gigs. So I do have to keep up with all the additions to my song list.

SET LISTS

---

*"Some songs, you just can't shake;
they keep creeping back
into your set list."*
—Lemmy (Motörhead)

I typically don't make set lists for solo acoustic shows, unless it is an all-original show at a venue for ticket sales or a radio appearance. Most of the time, in bars, restaurants, or private party settings, I will just use my judgment to mentally scroll through my song list and pick what I think will work based on the demographics of the audience or their requests.

Now, while I am great at taking requests, I do not know every song out there. One of the best things to do in a situation where someone asks you for a song that you don't know, is to propose another song by the same artist, in the same genre, or the same style. Another tool for appeasing someone who is requesting a song is to ask them if they want a happy song, or a sad song, or something bluesy, etc... Moving a specific request to something a little more vague can allow you to redirect it and pick out a song that you are really good at.

The standard pattern for a set list usually goes something like this. Start off with a series of upbeat and up-tempo songs, building to a "peak" or climax about mid-set. Then you can drop in one or two ballads or slower songs for the "valley" and begin to build the dynamics back up through volume and tempo, arriving at another peak for the end of the set.

I like to keep a few premade set lists in my book, which I can add to anytime. I start with labeling them by genres and filling them up with songs in that category. Then I will rearrange them a few times to find a really good flow in the order of keys, tempos, and lyrical content. I can use the app OnSong to create and save set/song lists on my ipad for different special occasions, events, or holidays. I can add to them each time I learn a song, or if I am requested to learn a specific song for an event. Then I am ready for the next time I play a similar gig.

I have blues, country, rock, reggae, '80s, Christmas, love song/ballad, and Fourth-of-July-themed set lists, plus a special Bob Marley set. His birthday is February 6, and I like to play a solid one-hour set of his songs in tribute to him at each one of my gigs that week.

I think you get the idea, and you can expand on these concepts with your own song choices.

SET TIMES

Set times are a much-discussed topic amongst my musician friends. There are several ways to think about this. The traditional 45-minute set with 15-20-minute breaks between has been around forever. Sometimes it's fun to change it up, and of course if you have a full bar that is vibing on what you are doing, you may want to play a long set to make more tips and keep them engaged. Other set times can be something like this: 60/30/60/30/60 minutes on a four-hour gig

Here are some examples of ways to break up a four-hour gig running from 6-10 PM:

6-6:45, 7:05-7:50, 8:10-8:55, 9:15-10 (45 minutes on, 20 minutes off)

6-7, 7:30-8:30, 9-10 (60 minutes on, 30 minutes off)

I have been known to use different patterns for sets depending on the gig. Here is one example that shows the sets getting shorter as the evening goes on and I am starting to have less energy: 6-7, 7:20-8:10, 8:30-9:10, 9:30-10.

Do you see how it works? A one-hour set, followed by a 50-minute set, a 40-minute set, and finally finishing the gig with a 30-minute set. This includes 20-minute breaks and offers the same amount of downtime as the other models.

One more example is this: 50/20, 50/20, 50/20, 30.

If the crowd is into what I am doing and I am getting really good energy from them, I have been known to play longer sets that can go for ninety minutes or more.

Now that I am using the OnSong app on my iPad, I can make a set list that is very easy to navigate. I will do this for special occasions. I recently did a gig where I was hired to play for an hour and a half. The catch was that they wanted only country songs. Using my iPad, I quickly picked out all the country songs in my book and made a set list. The reason for the chosen style of music was that Sun Country Airlines was making their inaugural flight from Tampa to Nashville out of TIA. They even had a cake that looked like a guitar! The body was yellow cake and the neck was chocolate cake, so I had two pieces of cake...

PRACTICE AND LEARNING NEW SONGS

While your goal may not be to become the next great virtuoso instrumentalist, you still need to practice consistently. Along with always being on time, always having backup gear, and all the other intangible things we can do to be better at our craft, practice can shield you against a lot of adversity. It really helps to feel confident in what you know you can and can't do on any given night. There are several old clichés that talk about always being able to do on stage what you did in practice. Rarely will you write new and exciting things on your instrument during a performance. Most of the time, these breakthroughs in your musical journey happen during practice sessions.

Here is a fun tip: practice playing the guitar blindfolded or with your eyes closed, and no cheating. You know, like in a kung fu movie where the student is training and the master puts a blindfold over their eyes. Get to know your fretboard. There are gigs where I close my eyes and envision my fretboard while I am playing. I have the choice to open my eyes at points of transitioning between notes or chords. Doing this stuff is fun for me, and it's also challenging to play my solo passages up and down the fretboard with my eyes closed.

Part of a Solo Acoustic Musician's job is to be familiar with their gear. So set up and play at home, before or between gigs, to explore new ideas on the microphone and your guitar. Loop pedals are a valuable resource for the Solo Acoustic Musician, so practicing and making new loops for new songs is pretty much a necessity. As you build your client base and start playing the same places regularly, you will be playing songs for the same owners, managers, employees, and regular customers. Living in a tourist area like I do brings new people to town all the time, but the local people are still the core of who you are playing for. So you need to always keep learning new songs and growing your skill set.

You can always get a guitar or voice teacher. These days, you can take lessons in several ways. Of course, in person at a music store or in someone's home is still the standard, and it is a highly effective form of hands-on training. But now, you can take lessons in real time or via tabs and videos online. There will be times when you will encounter several different tab/chord charts or play-through videos of the same song. You will have to filter through them to see which versions seem to work for you.

I have developed a system for learning new songs on a consistent basis. Every now and then I will have to do more and work harder to learn a new song, but this process seems to work for me.

The first thing I do is to look up tabs and chord charts on the Ultimate Guitar Tabs website. Not everything I find there is correct, and I often have to adjust the charts. I have found tabs that show an A chord, only to figure out it is really an Am7 chord. I have lots of examples of this type of thing. It also happens in the lyrics! So make sure you do your due diligence and double-check things. It is always possible that the person who transcribed the chords and lyrics got it wrong. You will also encounter versions with different keys or capo positions. You will need to find the version or shift the key to fit your vocal abilities.

The second step of my process is to get onto YouTube and search "how to play (name of song)" and explore the videos people have posted of themselves, teaching us how to play the song. Just like the tab sites, you will find different versions and arrangements of the song you want to learn. I like to watch several different versions to see which one is closest to what I believe is right. Most of the time I try to find simplified versions, to get a grasp of the basic chord chart. Adding in signature riffs and chord voicings comes next.

The third step is also done on YouTube. I look up any live video footage of the actual artist who wrote or performed the song. Hopefully I can find a solo acoustic version, where I can see the artist's hands and watch them play their song correctly. If I can't find a solo acoustic version, then I can watch a live band version. Even if the singer doesn't play an instrument, I still hope to be able to watch the guitar player and see the way the song is really played.

My fourth step is to get the chord chart and lyric sheet together in the way I like to see it in my book. I usually place the title, artist, and chord chart at the top of the page. Sometimes I will add the chords to the bridge to the right of that section's lyrics. It comes down to spacing; I want as much of the information I need as possible on one page. I used to print them out and put them in my giant binder, but these days I move them into Dropbox and transfer them into my iPad and onto my songbook app. The app can hold far more songs than a physical book, so I don't have to choose which songs go into my book and which need to come out to make room for newer ones.

This is a basic approach to the process of learning a song and getting it ready for a live performance. You can create your own process and find out what works best for you. I like a mix of old-school learning and new-school technology. When I was getting started, I would have to play and rewind tapes to try to figure out songs by ear. The alternative back then was to save up and buy the actual songbook at the record store. You can still find these in most of the music stores. Just to learn one hit song would require buying the official chord, tab, and lyric songbook of the whole album for about twenty dollars. Then I would have music for a whole album, even though I just wanted to learn one song. Today I am very happy to have all these new tools to help me sort through all the information and learn new songs quickly.

CREATE YOUR OWN SET LISTS

A musician friend of mine was playing a gig when another local musician came into the bar and was hanging out, watching his set. They are both about the same age and play some of the same venues around town. On a break, they exchanged pleasantries as they happened to already know each other.

Fast-forward a few weeks, and the first musician pops in on the second musician at one of his gigs. To his surprise, the second musician had completely stolen a medley of his. Nowadays it's called a mash-up. The second musician copied the first musician's ideas and played the same songs in the same order. This kind of upset the first musician, because he thought that they were friends. He was shocked that the second musician would just rip off his ideas.

Playing the same songs as other musicians is going to happen, and there is no way or reason to prevent it. It's just part of the job. But I don't think it's very nice to straight-up steal someone else's set, song for song, in the same order. There are so many songs to choose from and make your own set lists or mash-up ideas. Every now and then I see someone on our shared circuit playing a song that I thought only I was playing. It is fun to see their interpretation because it will

23

always be a little different than my version. It's also fun to chat with them about it when they go on break.

ADULT CONTENT

As I've said, my song list has hundreds of songs on it of all genres, moods, and types. I do have some adult content and comedy songs that I only play in appropriate situations. When I say adult content, I am referring to songs that have lyrics that discuss sex, drugs, and violence, or contain profanity. I will not sing these songs when there are children present or the possibility of them being in earshot. Although marijuana is finally becoming mainstream and legal, I won't sing songs about it when I am in front of kids. Part of reading the crowd and knowing what songs will work is guessing that certain songs may be inappropriate to play even when kids aren't obviously present.

I really don't want to offend anyone if I can help it, which is a tough task. One rule of thumb is that if the venue doesn't serve food, then most of the time there are no children present. The main point is that I have so many other songs to play and can make choices to only play adult songs at certain places and at certain times. I won't usually play a bunch of adult songs in the first set. These kinds of songs usually go over better during the late-night show or the last set of a nighttime gig. Another reason it works better in the later set is that people have had a few drinks and loosened up. This will usually put them in the mood to laugh at a silly song or two.

Over the years, I have been encouraged by the owners or managers of a handful of places to play adult songs. It can be fun and accepted in certain places. I used to do it more often, and now it is something I do more sparingly. Honestly, I believe it makes it a little more fun because I don't do it all the time. A lot of the adult song choices I have made are intended to make people laugh. I have also found some "clean" comedy songs that I can use in front of any audience. I think this is helpful for me because I get to use my humor skills at any show if I think it is the right time. I like to make people laugh and finding non-adult songs that are funny to sing has only added to my repertoire.

 **GEAR AND ACCESSORIES**

"It was my love for the guitar that first got me into music and singing."
—Ed Sheeran

GUITARS AND STRINGS

Everybody likes different styles and brands of guitars, for many different reasons. Most musicians even become "brand loyal" after using the same gear for a long time. The guitar I have been playing on all of my gigs for more than fifteen years is a Martin DC-15E. This is my main guitar and it has been a workhorse in my toolbox. It has all the scratches, dings, and the wear and tear that come from playing hundreds of gigs a year.

I actually purchased this Martin guitar after I played and beat up a Taylor for years and years of gigs. After about eight years of shows, the frets were very beaten down and I had a few fret buzz issues. (Fret buzz is one of the most common problems that guitarists face; it is one of many undesirable phenomena that can occur on a guitar or similar stringed instrument. Fret buzz occurs when the vibrating part of one or more strings physically strikes the frets that are higher than the fretted note or open note. There are many causes of uneven frets. Older guitars can warp and the frets can rise. Changes in temperature or humidity can also warp the fingerboard, causing frets to rise, which is especially true in acoustics. While it isn't the prettiest sound in the world, it's not unfixable.)

I was gigging all the time and the store luthier said he needed a week to get it repaired with new frets and a neck adjustment. It was a busy store in the Baltimore area that I had been going to for a long time. I trusted the guy and I was willing to wait. I didn't really have much choice, because he was backed up with guitars to work on. He knew me from past visits and actually bumped me up in the order because he knew I was a full-time working Solo Acoustic Musician. To cover all my gigs and make sure I didn't lose any work, I had to buy a guitar. I walked around the store checking out all of the acoustic guitars on the wall. I played a few different ones and just gravitated towards the Martin that has been with me ever since.

I also have my old Taylor as a backup guitar. I mostly use that in different alternate tunings to explore fun new ideas around the house. It can be helpful for songwriting to have some different feels and tones to find new inspirations. It has a deeper and fatter neck than my Martin, and it takes me a minute to readjust to it. I don't like to use this Taylor guitar on gigs anymore unless I have a volume pedal on my pedal board, because it does not have an active EQ on it, making it prone to volume swells unless I use my L.R. Baggs preamp to control the EQ and volume. Volume swells are a form of low-frequency feedback. When I am holding a low note in a chord, it can build up with sustain and continue to grow. I want to avoid that by implementing a volume control and/or an EQ. My Martin has a Fishman pre-amp EQ with a volume knob on it, and does not have this same problem in a live setting.

I also think it's a necessity for any Solo Acoustic Musician to have a third guitar that does not plug in or have any electronics at all. Think of your first beginner guitar, something inexpensive that you can take anywhere and play songs. A guitar you can take to the pool, the beach, climb a tree, go camping, etc. You don't have to worry about losing work if this guitar takes a tumble and hits the ground. That doesn't mean you have to beat it up on purpose, and as a matter of fact it's awesome to have a less expensive guitar set up by a luthier and to keep quality strings on it so it plays well and sounds great!

I lived in Colorado during the late nineties and would regularly go out camping with my "take anywhere" or "knock around" guitar. I used to go up on a mountain, build a fire, and play songs all night while looking down at the valley and the city lights below. During that time I was driving a 1969 VW camper van and it was great for sleeping out in the wild. Many nights were spent playing music by the fire and enjoying the crisp mountain air. Nowadays I use it around the house, sitting at my picnic table, hanging out by the pool, sitting around the campfire pit, relaxing on the beach, or going for a hike in one of our many local parks.

The last guitar is not one I actually have yet. This is the guitar I want to get my hands on and play. I have been very happy with my Taylor and my Martin for many years. Now I want to try a Cole Clark guitar. This company is located in Melbourne, Australia. I have looked up their availability in the

States, and they are unfortunately not being sold in Florida yet. I am sure I will get to play one sometime soon, anyway.

So my advice to you is to always have a fourth type of guitar on your horizon. Take a look at different brands. Check out the artists who endorse their products or those the company has sponsored. That might help you settle on a couple of possibilities out of hundreds of guitar companies. I enjoy the music of several musicians who are sponsored by and who endorse Cole Clark guitars, and that has helped spark my interest in playing one of their instruments.

When it comes to strings, I have probably tried all the brands over the years. I mostly play a Martin acoustic-electric guitar, so I think that the Martin Lifespan strings are a great match. I have also really grown fond of Elixir Nanoweb and Polyweb strings. Of the three I just mentioned, I have found that the Polywebs last the longest before needing to be replaced. These three are also on the higher end of pricing when it comes to buying strings, but I like to pamper myself with expensive strings and I can spend ten to twenty dollars a week on them. I cannot afford a new guitar every week, but I can buy a new pack of strings every week. It always sounds and feels better to me to have new strings on my guitar. If I feel good about the way my guitar is playing and sounding, then I give a better performance.

I don't really haggle with store employees on prices, but most managers give me some kind of deal when I buy one or two cases at a time. A case is a box of twelve packs of strings, and the savings add up over time. I also find that I get a discount for buying multiple packs or cases when ordering strings online. I prefer to buy my supplies from the local stores, though, to help them stay open. I appreciate my local music store way more than just getting on my computer and clicking some buttons. It's always fun to make a trip to the store and see what's going on in person.

What gauge of strings you use is also a personal preference. You should learn your guitar factory preset for the gauge though. For example, Martin is 0.12 gauge and a Fender Stratocaster is a 0.09 gauge preset. When you buy a new guitar, have it set up for the gauge you like to use, or you can damage your instrument if it is not set for the factory preset. For example, if the preset is 0.12 and you are using 0.13, then over time you may warp the body or hurt the neck. The tension will be too much for what your guitar is set up for.

PA EQUIPMENT

Buy quality equipment and learn how to use it. About two years ago I downsized and upgraded all at once by making one purchase. I bought a 200 watt Compact XL manufactured by AER Amps out of Germany. This amp is small and only weighs about twenty-two pounds. I still can't believe the amount of sound and volume that I can get out of this magic little box. I can play any size room or outdoor venue with this amp and I only add a speaker if I am required to have an extra one for an indoor/outdoor setup (meaning I'm actually playing inside, but the owner wants a speaker outside to draw in foot traffic from the street).

My AER amp was expensive, at just under two thousand dollars, but it was worth every penny. I don't know how the company did it, but it has the best sound of any amp or PA system I have ever used. It is crystal clear for both guitar and vocals. I swear they sprinkled some kind of magic fairy dust on the components inside! Every musician who hears me playing through it is amazed. Now, when I play a festival stage with a soundman, I can have a little more control of my stage sound, because it acts as a monitor for me and sounds just like I do at all my gigs, so I don't have to worry about what the sound guys are doing for my monitor mix.

I still have some older PA gear ready on standby in case I need it for any reason. This setup includes three Mackie 1000-watt thumper powered speakers and an Alesis mixer. If you can afford to buy backup gear, do it. I like to keep three powered speakers in my arsenal just in case one malfunctions. This way I always have another to use in a two-speaker setup while the broken one is being repaired. It is very important to buy quality equipment, purchase the repair protection if you can, and know your manufacturer's warranty.

You will also want to find a local repair shop with a good reputation. Asking other local musicians for advice can be helpful. I have used the same repair shop many times for different equipment of different brands and they have always treated me well, with attention to detail and a quick turnaround time. Now, I do know several musicians who do not like that same company because of issues in the past. I have not experienced the same negative outcomes and still go to that same repair company when needed.

MICROPHONE

There are several standard $100 microphones on the market and they are going to work great. You don't have to spend $500 on a mic, but you don't want to purchase a $30 mic either. I use a $100 Sennheiser microphone and have an identical backup in my guitar case if I need it.

Remember to always buy two: you are going to need a microphone and microphone cables. In the case of XLR mic cables, I keep four on hand. Some places where I play want me to run into their house system, from the back of my amp into an XLR input box on the wall. So, I make sure I have a couple extra ones handy. Also, when I am playing at a private party or corporate function, they may want to use a microphone to make an announcement or speech. I ask about this when I arrive, and if they would like to use a mic, I will set one up off to the side. This way I don't have to unwrap mine from the mic stand. This also means I can control their channel mix separately from mine, so I don't accidentally change anything on my channel.

FOOT PEDALS

While you don't need any foot pedals at all, I like to keep a few basics on the floor to enhance my show. There are many different pedal functions and brands to purchase. You will have to experiment with them to find the ones you like to use. My pedal board always has three basic tools:

A tuner pedal, which also acts as a mute for my guitar between songs and on break (Boss Tu-3, $100)

A single-channel loop station (Boss RC-1, $100)

A delay pedal (Boss-3, $100)

Sometimes I use two delays that are set differently, and sometimes I add a volume pedal for volume swells. I have tried distortion and wah-wah pedals, but I don't like the way they sound with an acoustic guitar. Foot pedals can add some spice and color to your sound and your songs, so have fun trying out different combos and see what you like to use for different feels. There are many options out there to investigate; I just try to keep it as simple as I can.

ACCESSORIES

Remembering that if you can, always buy two of everything; here is a list of odds and ends that will be needed on the job. Some of the items will be needed often, and some will come in handy once in a while. These are all just tools in the box.

Guitar Stand: I only use my guitar stand on high-end gigs. You know, the ones where there is a nice stage or I am required to wear dress clothes. For these types of gigs, I like to hide my guitar case from view and stash it somewhere off the stage area. Sometimes this means I take my guitar case, amp case, pedal board case, and my cart all the way back to the van. I like to keep a clean and neat stage to work on.

Otherwise, at my casual bar and restaurant gigs I just put my guitar back in the case when I am on break. I live in Florida and it is always very humid, so I like to put my guitar in the case instead of in the open air on a guitar stand, especially when I am playing outside near the water.

Duct Tape: Buy black duct tape for taping down cables on stage. I mostly use it when I have to run an extension cord across a walkway and want to make sure it's taped down for safety reasons. If it is possible to find a small piece of carpet to cover the extension cord and tape, that would be the most aesthetically pleasing way to go. Black gaffer tape is also acceptable for covering cables for safety. It is usually more expensive than duct tape, but it can be removed more cleanly. It's probably best to keep both on hand, as they have different capabilities while sharing similar purposes.

Extension Cords: I keep a couple of ten-footers on my pedal board. I also keep a couple of twenty-five-foot and fifty-foot cords in the van. It doesn't happen often, but every now and then I may need one hundred feet of cord to reach a power outlet.

String Winder: I don't break strings often, but when I do I am prepared to handle the situation. This tool costs about $1 on the counter at the music store. It speeds up the time it takes to change a string and can really help in a live setting. It only takes me about two minutes to change a string out and get back to playing. I have a system, and my tools and spare strings are right in my case. I just stay calm, do not rush, and it is an easy fix.

Bridge Pins: One thing that could cause a problem in my string-changing routine is accidentally dropping or popping out a bridge pin. They are very small and can disappear easily. If this happens, I will only look for it for a little bit because I keep extra ones in a small ziploc bag in my guitar case. You never know when you might need one.

Needle-Nose Pliers: Keep these on hand to cut the strings when you are taking them off and replacing them with new ones. They are also used to trim off the excess string at the tuning peg.

Fans: I have two fans that also have electric outlets on them. This means they have a double purpose, because they also serve as extension cords. Even when I play inside in an air-conditioned venue, I will bring in and set up my fans. I may not have them on, but they are part of my setup now.

Mic Stand Drink Holder: I place this high enough on my mic stand that I can drink from my cup through a straw in the middle of a song. I see other Solo Acoustic Musicians using the same type of drink holder, but they have placed it at waist level and can only pick up their drink between songs. Have you ever started coughing in the middle of a song and really needed a sip of water? That is why I keep my drink holder up high...

Capo: I always keep two of these in my case. I rarely use them but I have them. Another local musician posted his location on Facebook and said that he needed a capo. I responded to him from a restaurant where I was playing that was only three blocks away. He ran down on his break and picked up the capo. When our gigs were over he ran back to return my capo—and gave me $10 for helping him out. So while I don't use a capo very often, just having one with me helped someone else.

Pedal Board Power Supply: Like I said, buy two! I always keep an extra pedal board power supply in my gear box in the van.

Batteries: My guitar has an active electronic EQ and volume system that runs off nine-volt batteries. So every now and then, the little red light comes on telling me that my battery is about to die. I have been told that when the light comes on I probably have an hour of battery power left before my guitar quits working. So I keep several extra nine-volt batteries in my guitar case at all times.

Guitar Picks: It's another no-brainer here. Keep some in your pocket, guitar case, car, and even inside your guitar. (That's right, drop a few into your guitar...)

Small Adapters: The XLR to 1/4", male-to-female or female-to-male adapters may be needed if the house system wall input is 1/4" and your main/line out is XLR, so keep some of these in your gear box or guitar case.

Tables: Small, cheap card tables. Get one for your picks, drinks, phone, keys, etc., and another for your tip can and/or merchandise display.

Slide: While I don't play slide guitar very often, I keep one in my guitar case, just in case I might decide to use it or another musician needs one. If you do use one, keep a spare in your guitar case.

Harmonica & Kazoo: I keep these around just for the fun of having noisemakers. I don't actually use them much, but it's fun when I do, and it always turns some heads.

Snark Tuner: I keep one of these for when I change strings or use a guitar around the house.

Cell Phone Chargers: I like to keep at least two on hand, in my guitar case. Sometimes people will ask me if I have a charger they can plug in to. Having one available can turn into a couple dollars in my tip can.

Koozies: I keep a couple koozies with me because some places I play provide bottled water. It's summertime weather in Florida year-round, so koozies are essential to keeping my water bottle cool.

ALWAYS BUY TWO

Whenever you go to the music store for supplies, always buy two of everything that you can afford to double up on, especially affordable accessories that you use a lot. Common examples would be strings, picks, capos, microphones, cables, string winders, batteries, and I would also include extension cords, bug spray, fans, towels, duct tape, etc. If you need to, make a list of your gear and accessories to determine what you think you need to have a backup for. I know not everyone can afford a backup guitar. So I try to make sure I can purchase backups for most everything else I need.

Another Solo Acoustic Musician friend of mine actually had two microphones stop working at the same gig. She had a backup microphone, but it failed too. Luckily I happened to be there and had an extra microphone in the van that she borrowed to get through the gig. This was a very rare occurrence all around... My gig was cancelled that night due to weather, so I went to a place on the way home where I like to go for a good dinner. They also have live music and I even play there as well from time to time. My friend was supposed to start at six, and it was fifteen minutes after the hour when she came over to ask me if I had an extra microphone she could borrow. I left her with the mic and returned around 10 PM, toward the end of her gig. She actually asked another friend to go to the liquor store and buy me a $25 bottle of tequila so she could surprise me with a gift to thank me for helping her out. I was very surprised, to say the least, and greatly appreciated the gesture. I have told that story to many other Solo Acoustic Musicians I have had the pleasure of meeting over the years.

Whenever I buy a guitar, I immediately drop extra guitar picks into the body through the sound hole. They make a little noise from time to time if you shake your guitar, but that rarely happens and doesn't bother me at all. I only find myself in a position to need them about twice a year, but every now and then I leave the house in a hurry and forget to put some picks in my pocket. I usually don't realize it until I get to where I am going. That's when I grin and turn my guitar over to dump a pick onto the floor. This little trick has saved me on more than one occasion, and I am sure it will bail me out a few more times in the future.

TRANSPORTATION AND ACCESSORIES

"What does music mean to me? I don't think I would really be much without it, without it coming through me. It's my means of communication, my means of growth, my means of transportation from one point of my life to another."
—Erykah Badu

I drive a Dodge Grand Caravan minivan due to gas mileage and cargo space. A sedan is great on gas mileage but does not have enough room for all of my gear. Even though I have scaled back my solo rig, a small car would not be optimal. As a Solo Acoustic Musician, a large van requires way more than I want to spend on gas, but is great for storing all of my equipment and pretty awesome if I want to bring friends to a gig or on a road trip. So my Dodge Grand Caravan minivan works great for me. I get the gas mileage and the space I need, all in one vehicle.

I also carry a few pieces of gear, which I will describe below.

Cart or Dolly: I have scaled down the PA that I use the most, which I described in the previous chapter. Now, all the gear that I need to perform a show will fit into one cart, and my guitar is in a rather large Gator brand backpack travel case. My Gator case can actually hold two guitars and lots of extras in its compartments. This enables me to make a long-distance walk load in with a single trip from the van to the stage area. This is great for me. I am saving time and effort!

Tarp: Depending on where you live and the time of year, you may encounter outdoor gigs that offer weather challenges for you to deal with. I never want to have a drop of water touch my gear! But if I have to play a gig in an environment where that is even a possibility, I like to have a plan as a last resort in case of a sudden downpour. So I keep a 10' x 12' tarp in the bottom of my cart, and I will leave my cart right next to, if not on, the stage area.

Pop-up Tent: While I do not keep a tent in my van, I ask the client to provide me with one for some outdoor bookings. It should go without saying that standing in the hot Florida sun for any amount of time, never mind more than four hours, and on top of that having the possibility of a pop-up rain storm looming here, you will want some kind of cover overhead. The weather in Florida is severely bipolar, and can go haywire really quickly and return to normal just as quickly. One of those superfast storms could be devastating to my equipment, and I try my best to avoid or be prepared for the possibility of a worst-case scenario.

I also try to always have extra clothes with me on gigs, and of course I change them out throughout the year depending on the season. When I lived in places that actually had cold weather, I adapted to winter situations as well. Keeping extra long-sleeved T-shirts, sweaters, and even a vest in the van for when it's cold is a smart thing to do.

When I moved to Florida, I learned very quickly that I might have to change my T-shirt once or even twice during a single afternoon gig. If it's a summer heat wave, I may have to change my shirt as many as four times. It gets extremely hot and humid here most of the year, and although weather may dictate some wardrobe choices, I also keep dress shirts on hangers in the van for dress-up gigs. Along with a stack of extra T-shirts and other clothing items, I always keep a soft couch-sized pillow, a blanket, two or three towels, and a few hats on the pile. Here in Florida, it helps to have at least one wide-brimmed hat to cover your ears and nose from the sunshine. All the essentials should be there, too: socks, boxers, flip-flops, sneakers, extra sunglasses...

"Stow-and-go" items are a separate discussion. I actually list all my stow-and-go items on paper and tape it to my visor. This way I can flip my visor down and know exactly what I have in the compartments of my van, including which side of the van each thing is kept on. The usual list includes another extra pair of flip-flops; an old songbook in case my iPad acts up; a tire air-pressure pump that plugs into my AC outlet; an extra electric outlet adapter with two wall inputs and two USB inputs that plugs into my AC outlet; and a one-gallon ziploc bag full of plastic silverware, wet wipes, and napkins.

We can also include the items stored in the vehicle's console, like a USB charging stick for emergency charging of your cell phone or tablet, Tums for your stomach, wet wipes, a first aid kit, and any other personal hygiene items. I even keep a toothbrush in a blue light case in a ziploc bag. Another issue related to living in Florida is that dealing with pollen is a constant struggle, so allergy pills of some kind usually find their way into the console at certain times of year.

CLEAN BATHROOMS

Always know where they are.

A lot of places I play do not keep their restrooms clean, and when you are out on the road it can be even worse. Know your neighborhoods...

I have memberships to a couple of chain gyms for exactly this purpose. Once a month, I play a place that I know has a horrible bathroom, but there's a gym about four doors down from the bar, where I am a member. While my home gym is closer to my house, I have a key fob that gets me into every location of this chain nationwide. So when I am at this particular gig and need to use the restroom, I just walk down the block on my break. If you are on the road and don't have a gym membership, you can usually buy a day pass to a local gym for $5. This will allow you to get some exercise and take a shower. Both can be a blessing when you are travelling in a van for three to nine hours a day for more than a week.

When I was on mini-tours with a couple of other Solo Acoustic Musicians, I used to point out to the others that the best, cleanest bathrooms could be found by reading signs on the highway. Mind you, I was not talking about gas stations, fast-food restaurants, or rest stops. I was talking about hospitals and high-end hotels. You can look for the big-name hotels on exit signs; they're readily available. Just walk through the lobby as if you belong there and look for the bathroom signs. They are usually off to the right or left, and always clean!

You should also keep a lookout for the blue square with a white H. Every hospital has a bathroom in a hallway that leads to a door to the outside, and they are required to be extremely clean due to infectious bacteria and germs. So you have a virtual guarantee of a clean place to use the facilities...

SECURITY

Always lock your doors!

Once, many years ago, another Solo Acoustic Musician—and also a friend—came by towards the end of my gig at a tiki bar in Ocean City, MD. He invited me to join him at a get-together at a mutual friend's condo by the beach. I threw my guitar next to his in the back of his Jeep Cherokee, and off we went to the party.

When we arrived, we hopped out and went up to the condo to check out the scene and grab a beer. After hanging out for about half an hour, we went back down to the parking lot to grab our guitars. We were going to play some songs on the balcony overlooking the moonlit ocean. When we opened the back of the Jeep, our guitars were gone! My friend kinda lost it when he realized he had not locked the door. It was a rather crappy ending to our evening, and it was a pretty quiet ride home that night.

The next day when I got up, it really hit me hard that my $3000 Taylor guitar was gone. I had worked a lot of gigs and saved a long time to buy that guitar. I had to try to salvage my day and get going to play another gig. Since that was my only guitar at the time, I called some friends and was able to borrow a guitar to play some gigs until I could buy another one when I had a day off to shop. To my surprise, on the way to a happy hour gig, my phone rang. The man on the other end of the line told me about two guitars that he and a friend had confiscated from two drunk kids the night before, and asked me if they were ours.

The story he told me was interesting. As he and his best friend were walking home from a bar, they were approached by two younger guys, who asked them if they would like to buy two guitars really cheap. He told me that they only asked for $50 for each guitar. It was at this point that they realized the guitars were probably stolen, and they told the guys to hand over the guitars and to beat it.

I interjected and told him I was on my way to a gig at the 17th Street Holiday Inn in Ocean City, Maryland. I offered to buy him and his friend food and drinks, and give them $100, if they would please bring our guitars to the tiki bar at the inside pool area. When they walked in with our guitars, I immediately knew why the thieves had surrendered the guitars so easily and ran off. These two men were about 6'6" each, and were bodybuilders with huge muscles. I handed them a hundred-dollar bill and introduced them to the bartender, asking her to give these gentlemen the VIP treatment and that I would pay for whatever they wanted.

Now, not every situation ends like this. I know several other musicians who have had gear stolen and never seen it again. I was very lucky this time and am forever grateful to a couple of really nice people who did the right thing. So always lock your doors.

There are other things you can do that may help you recover stolen gear. I had my receipt and my business card in my case, so these two guys saw the value of my guitar and also had my contact information. Always put your business card in your case, and even leave one inside of your acoustic guitar (yes, with the picks). It also helps if you can put a unique marking on the inside of your guitar that only you know about, like branding a cow. It also can't hurt to take some photos of your instrument or gear with your smartphone and send them to cloud storage. Pictures of you wearing a particular guitar on CD covers, posters, your website, and all your social media pages can also be used to prove ownership of your gear to the police, if necessary, after your equipment has been sold or pawned and recovered.

You should always be aware of your surroundings in general. As a SAM, I work alone, and that means that I don't have other band members hanging around the van when I am loading in or loading out. At home or at the venue, I will do things in stages if I need to. This means that on every trip from the van to the stage or into my house I completely close and lock my van. In years past, when it would take me two to four trips, depending on how much gear I was carrying, I would close and lock my vehicle on every trip.

I have heard stories of musicians leaving the back door of their van open while carrying in some equipment. Sometimes they might get delayed or distracted by a curious patron. Even if they don't, and they travel straight to the stage and back, it doesn't take long for a passerby to grab some of your gear and take off. There are even thieves who hang around bars looking for opportunities. This is a particular issue if the street has multiple live-music venues close to each other. That creates an atmosphere that is ripe for a thief to catch a musician off guard.

I want to protect my house, my family, my gear, and my transportation from theft or damage. I have had to unload and get into the house in the country, the suburbs, and the city. Each time I have moved or lived in a new city, I have had to learn as much as possible about the neighborhood. With each new apartment or roommate situation comes a different set of circumstances. I will still play and sing, but I have to adapt to new environments and people. Once again, it's part of the lifestyle that you will grow accustomed to.

When I was younger I took a lot more chances about leaving my gear in the car. I learned the hard way. I changed my behavior and made sure that I created routines and put systems in place to prevent problems as much as possible.

I also recommend that you not advertise that you are a SAM. What I mean by this is, do not advertise your business on the side of your car or van like a birthday clown or other act might do. I have seen people do it, whether they are a solo act or a band, and I don't think it is very smart. You are telling potential thieves that valuable music equipment is inside your vehicle. I also don't see any professional upside to placing your name and logo on the side of your vehicle. You should already be doing enough promotion for your act with emails, texts, and social media. I really don't think a magnet, a sticker, or a painted-on sign will help in any way.

 # HEALTH AND NUTRITION

"All the money in the world can't
buy you back good health."
—Reba McEntire

It's important to address this subject because we all want to look and feel our best on stage. So if you were wondering why health and nutrition was in this book, now you know.

The first thing to consider, when you're trying to stay healthy as a SAM, is washing your hands. Washing my hands at the bar on breaks during gigs, and especially when coming home after a gig, is very important. Bars and restaurants are full of surfaces, doorknobs, menus, and strangers who want to shake my hand. Let's begin with the idea that no place I play washes their menus. As a SAM, you are likely to run into this issue as well. It's something most people don't even think about, but now that I've told you that, you'll never be able to get it out of your head. (Sorry!) My advice is to memorize the menu at places you play frequently, and know what each spot has available and which choices suit your dietary needs.

When I get home from a gig I unload my gear from the van and into the house, take off my shoes, and then wash my hands. This one small step helps me avoid getting a cold or the flu when it's going around the restaurants and bars. Nothing can shield me from one hundred percent of the germs that I encounter on a daily basis, but washing my hands regularly does increase my chances of staying healthy. Sometimes when I am on a gig I prefer to do fist bumps instead of shaking hands, especially when I see lots of other musicians posting on social media that they are sick.

"Music has a healing power.
It has the ability to take people out of
themselves for a few hours." —Elton John

There are two books on health that I recommend you read. There are lots of health books and dietary literature out there, but I have spent time with these two and they made a difference in my life. That is the only reason I am going to share them with you. They are *The 4-Hour Body* by Timothy Ferriss, and *The Singer's Guide To Complete Health*, edited by Anthony F. Jahn, MD.

Cardio exercises are great for your singing voice! Singing is all about breathing, and doing any kind of cardio workout will help you improve or maintain your singing ability. I have said it a few times already that many things in this book are common sense. Go for a run, take a bike ride, or jump in the pool for a swim. Even going for a short walk while listening to music is a great way to maintain a little bit of cardio. When I choose to walk, I focus on breathing. I just try to stay active so I feel good and perform at my best.

There are two basic health-related factors that I try to control when I am on a gig: food and drink. I try to eat and drink healthy items when I am playing and singing. I drink water or unsweetened tea and I try to have a small side or house salad if I eat before I start playing, or when I go on a break. I do like to take a nice dinner home at the end of some gigs. A few places where I perform regularly give me a meal as part of my compensation. I will typically get a chicken or salmon dinner with rice, and broccoli or asparagus. Not every place that I work with provides me with food, so sometimes I will pack a snack. Most of the time it is nothing more than a banana or an apple.

Quite often the food on the road or in bars and some restaurants might not be the best choice for me, so I plan ahead and bring a small cooler if necessary, to provide myself with better options. This also goes a long way with food requirements when dealing with places that do not provide a meal or even have food available. I often perform at breweries, which do not have a kitchen at all. Although some are working in conjunction with food trucks, there are no guarantees that one will be on site at the time I am there, or that if one is there, that their menu will be agreeable to me.

I sometimes play at a large hotel in my area that has an employee cafeteria with everything you could possibly want. Even though there are healthy options, it can be a struggle not to grab a slice of pizza, a hot dog, and a piece of cake. I usually try to have a salad with a small amount of protein instead. I don't like to feel gassy or bloated on stage, and I prefer to eat a bigger meal after I am done with my show.

A lot of places I have played over the years have provided me a meal, but one that really stood out was a cheesesteak I ordered in Altoona, PA. I asked for lettuce and onion on my sandwich. The bartender brought me a cheesesteak that had little bits of carrots and radish in it. I guess the cook must have used a bagged salad mix to get the lettuce when he was making my sub. It was a heavy metal bar, and I didn't really fit in as a performer... or a patron, for that matter. I never played there again, but I will always remember that cheesesteak.

I like to use tea, lozenges, and candy on gigs to keep my throat from drying out and to stay comfortable when I am singing. Throat Coat by Traditional Medicinals is an organic, naturally caffeine-free herbal tea. Try adding lemon and honey when you can. They also make this tea with lemon echinacea in it, which is good for immune system support. Fisherman's Friend is the best cough drop in the world. I have been using them on gigs for years and have also recommended them to other Solo Acoustic Musicians. If I am at someone else's gig and I hear them cough, I go over and offer them a Fisherman's Friend.

Tic-Tacs are also another great tool for keeping my mouth moist and my breath fresh. I have fun with Tic-Tacs and engage the crowd by telling them that the next song I am going to play is sponsored by Tic-Tac. People always laugh and it's a good icebreaker for me with the audience.

I once played three-on-three basketball with Tim McGraw at the Delaware State Fair. He brings a portable basketball hoop with him in the gear truck. (At least he used to years ago.) It's the first thing out of the truck and the last thing into the truck after the show. I was twenty-two at the time and I was moonlighting with stagehand work in between gigs. It was a $20/hour job lifting boxes, and included a meal and a concert. On this night, an added bonus was getting to play a pickup game of basketball with a famous country musician.

All the guys in his crew had their own ways of staying in shape on the road. One of the guitar players told me he liked to walk or ride a bike around the concourses of the stadiums and arenas they played. Musicians often have to be creative to stay healthy while working an ever-changing schedule that's never nine-to-five. My lifestyle includes early and late shifts on varying days of the week; my schedule is in a constant state of change, so it's important to be able to deal with that and go with the flow.

Getting health insurance is very important. It does cost money out of my pocket, as an independent contractor running my own small business. But there are affordable plans out there, and it can really save the day if you get the flu or need to see an ear, nose, and throat doctor. My health insurance does not cover dental visits and I usually just pay out-of-pocket for cleanings. If I ever do need expensive dental work, there are dental financing companies out there.

RESTING MY VOICE

First of all let me clarify that I really try to never hurt my voice. This means that when I go to a concert or sporting event, I never yell and scream. I always choose to clap loudly and save my voice. I try not to yell at all. I have heard people talking on Monday after watching football all day on Sunday and yelling at their television. Their voices are hoarse and scratchy. Or maybe they were at a bar, talking to friends over loud music and crowd noise. I avoid doing either of these things. I do find myself in these environments from time to time, but I just choose not to talk loudly over all the noise. Hopefully I don't overdo it when I am out with my friends having fun somewhere loud.

It can be hard not to wear down over time by just singing a lot. I have to stay hydrated by drinking water and lots of Throat Coat tea. After singing six nights a week for months on end, the wear and tear can add up. I find that one thing is the most important: resting my voice. A good night's sleep can help, but it is also good to talk as little as possible when healing up your voice. Sometimes I will go days without talking at all. I carry a pen in my front pocket and a folded piece of paper in my back pocket. I also almost always have a clipboard with paper on it in my van everywhere I go.

When I go into a restaurant for lunch or dinner I will use my piece of paper to communicate with the waiter or bartender. The same thing works at the produce stand or grocery store. I really don't need to talk much in those situations, but if I have my pen and paper with me, I don't have to talk at all. With email and text messages, I can handle a lot of business without talking at all on my resting days. I can check in with family and friends the same way, so those two tools are very valuable.

I actually like talking to people all the time, so remaining silent becomes quite a challenge for me. I like to make it a game and really try not talking for a whole day. Believe it or not, I have gone three days in a row with no talking. I didn't have any gigs and it was actually pretty fun to just shut up. When I am in resting mode, I do still have to talk on gigs, so that is an exception. I have to converse with employees of the venues, and of course the audience. I can still manage to avoid overdoing it by not talking a lot on my breaks, though.

There is an added perk to resting my voice. That is that people just seem to be nicer to me when I am writing notes to communicate with them. I am not pretending to be mute, but

I am not sure if they assume that I can't talk. I am sure people who are sick or have laryngitis experience this same thing.

Most professional athletes have seasons, and play a certain number of games each year. They have the "off-season" to rest and train. Also, they usually have teammates who play the same amount of game time that they do. Most professional musicians that play concerts and go on tour will play twenty to fifty shows a year. I could list a bunch of famous bands and write out their schedules but it's not necessary. I find it fun to count the shows when I see someone wearing a famous band's T-shirt with the tour schedule on the back. It's usually about thirty-five dates over a summer tour. For the most part, the band will play one hour to two hours straight for their set.

As a SAM, I will play four to six gigs a week. Each one of these gigs will be three to four hours long. I don't have teammates to sub in for me when I get tired. I don't have a coach or a manager to help me navigate through the tough times, so I just have to stay strong and show up on time and give my best every night, all the time. It's a marathon, and I have to pace myself. I will play when I'm sick, I will play when I'm hurt, I will sing with a sore throat, I will play every show I can so that I can make a living. Some venue managers and owners are understanding about what I go through.

"I've never missed a gig yet. Music makes people happy, and that's why I go on doing it—I like to see everybody smile."
—Buddy Guy

One morning in the summer of 2008 I woke up at about 8:45 AM and was getting ready to head to the bank to get a cashier's check for the rent. I had two roommates at the time and our apartment complex office did not want three separate payments. So every month I would collect the money, consolidate it at the bank, and turn the payment in to the complex office. I walked into the pool area and headed for the soda machine to buy a Coke. As I turned around, I slipped on a wet spot on the pool deck and fell. My right hand which was holding the soda, hit the ground.

My hand immediately swelled up and I went back to my apartment. It was pretty obvious that my hand was broken. I went to the hospital, where they took X-rays and put me in a cast. It was a spiral fracture in my fifth metacarpal bone and would take months to heal. These kinds of breaks are known as boxer's fractures because they usually happen when you punch something, which is pretty much what happened when I landed. I didn't mean to punch the ground, but basically I did.

At the time I was playing six days a week and I did not have anywhere near enough savings to take ten weeks off while I wore a cast. So I did every gig wearing a full cast. I had limited mobility and only the use of my thumb and index finger on my right hand. It was just enough to hold my guitar pick. My load-ins were interesting to say the least. I would wear my sling and do everything left-handed. I was using a Mackie powered mixer and two Yamaha speakers at the time. The speakers were fifteen inches with a horn and weighed about ninety pounds each. I had to set up the speaker stands and lift the speakers up one-handed. Believe me, it was a challenge—but I did it, six days a week.

I would hear people talking in the crowd as I was setting up, and some folks just straight up asked me, "Are you going to play with a cast on?" I always replied, "Yes. I have bills to pay." I definitely had a short adjustment period; it's awkward to play guitar with your hand in a cast. But in the end I adapted and made it through every gig successfully. Thankfully I have not had another experience as drastic as that one, but I have definitely had to get through gigs when I didn't feel well.

"I love to play music. So why endanger that with
something like drugs?"
—Dave Grohl

Many of us like to drink alcoholic beverages and I am one of them. I am not going to preach very hard on the subject of not drinking or getting drunk on gigs, because it took me a long time to stop doing it. But there is more than one reason to avoid alcohol on a gig.

I will start with one that took some research to understand, after it happened to me a few times. I was playing a winery and singing very well all throughout the first one-hour set. I decided to have a glass of red wine on my break. At some point during my second set, I lost my voice. I mean I could barely talk in a rough, scratchy voice. I didn't know what the heck was going on. I thought that maybe I was worn out from singing too much, or maybe my throat was dry from the wine, so I chugged a couple of glasses of water. It did not help.

On the second gig I booked at that winery, the same thing happened. I did not know what to think. I had to stop singing and pack up again halfway through a gig. I was puzzled by the situation. So I went home and did some research. I called some friends, I went online, and finally came to the conclusion that their particular red wines had a high sulfite content that was actually affecting my voice, and therefore my performance and my wallet. I obviously wanted to make changes.

The third (and believe it or not, last) time I played a gig at that winery I did not drink their wine and I sang very well all night, just as I had done before and after every other time I was there. I strictly drank water and performed very well. I made it through the gig, was paid for my time and efforts, and then went home to relax. I felt I had learned something. I still share that story with other musicians if the topic comes up. I used to always think that wine, and red wine in particular, was good for singing. I was wrong, and I learned a valuable lesson.

Another reason to not drink on stage is that beer makes me burp. I can imagine that your response is to think that I am silly or crazy. But it is uncomfortable to have to hit a note while needing to burp at the same time.

Drinking a little bit on stage can add to a party atmosphere, but being visibly drunk on stage can make you seem unprofessional. I have made this mistake many times in the past, but have grown past it and am better off for it. These days I prefer to perform completely sober and I really enjoy my experiences on stage. I may have a few drinks on a day off with friends or at home, and that seems to work better for me. I am not telling any of you potential Solo Acoustic Musicians what to do. I am simply sharing my experiences based on the years of gigs I have played. Some of them were enhanced by alcohol, but I know some of them were train wrecks because of alcohol.

On a few occasions, I have actually had to call, email, text, or ask in group forums for someone to cover my shift because I was so hungover and sick that I couldn't actually go perform a gig. I am in a happy place in my life where that doesn't happen anymore. I am going to tell you that it didn't happen much in my twenties, but it did start catching up with me in my thirties, and now in my forties I know better and it doesn't cost me gigs, money, or professional respect.

I have always planned to sing and play my guitar until the day I die. I would like to think I have quite a few years left to perform in front of people. By managing my schedule, staying in shape, building my network, and learning new songs, I believe I can last a long time as a SAM. I know a few full-time SAMs who are in their early to mid-twenties and have one to three years of full-time experience under their belt. I hope that they can figure out how to sustain a long career as a SAM. Planning for your future as a SAM is important. I can already look back and note some milestones. I remember when I became confident enough to ask for a little more money than I had previously been paid. It took planning and time for me to put myself in a position where I was able to step up my game and get a little more money. I will constantly try to think of ways that I can improve what I do, so that I can last longer and keep playing music for a living.

Musicians don't retire;
they stop when there's no more music in them.
—Louis Armstrong

 # SONGWRITING

---

*"[You] don't really go to songwriting school; you
learn by listening to tunes. And you try to understand
them and take them apart and see what they're
made of, and wonder if you can make one, too."*
—Tom Waits

There are lots of ways to write songs. Sometimes a song just flows right out of me all at once, and in very short order the music, the lyrics, and the arrangement all fall into place. Other times it may take three years to finish a song. I have learned that most of the time it's about recognizing inspiration and focusing on making some notes that can lead to lyrical ideas when I have time to follow up. I keep a piece of paper and a pen on me at all times. I never know when I am going to get a new idea for a song, or new thoughts on a song that is in the process of being written.

I seem to get into writing songs in batches—I will get inspired, get on a roll, and end up writing several songs at the same time. This doesn't mean that the songs are about the same topic or related to each other at all. It also doesn't mean that the songs are in the same style or genre. I just find myself being creative, and gaining energy as I work. There are times when I just write one song. But I have noticed that it usually leads to more, which is great because I really don't like to force it.

The flip side of writing songs in batches is that afterward, I need to reload my inspiration. I often tell friends about this in one of a few ways. One, I guess I need to get into a six-week relationship so that I can write the next album. Two, it's like when you are washing your car and your sponge gets dry, so you have to let it sit in the bucket and soak up water before you can continue to wash. Three, it's like when a wizard casts a spell to kill a giant demon who is trying to kill him and his friends, but then he is too drained of his strength and power to continue. These are just a few ways to describe the need to recharge one's inspiration in order to write new songs.

People say inspiration can come from the oddest places, and that is completely true. I can listen to songs on the radio and have no idea what inspired the artist to write those lyrics and place them with that music. Every one of us finds inspiration in our own way. I will once again suggest that you never force creativity, but try to pay attention and if an inspired thought arrives, try to act on it. Maybe jot down a note or get out your guitar and start going for it.

"I don't force it. If you don't have an idea and you don't hear anything going over and over in your head, don't sit down and try to write a song. You know, go mow the lawn... My songs speak for themselves."
—Neil Young

The majority of the songs I write come from personal experiences as well as my imagination. I have written many love songs using my imagination and pretending that I was in love. It has been a great exercise for me and I believe it has helped me write some pretty good songs.

One song that I wrote like this is called "Tides." The song itself took three years to finish. I wrote the first verse and the chorus the first time I sat down to work on it. After playing the music many times and trying to write more verses, I added an instrumental intro. I finally wrote a second verse three years later and the song was complete: three minutes and six seconds that I am still very proud of.

"I wish I were one of those people who wrote songs quickly. But I'm not. So it takes me a great deal of time to find out what the song is."
—Leonard Cohen

I am not the best at writing from an objective point of view, but I have some friends who excel at it. This means that they observe life and write about people and situations. Some of them have told me how they choose a topic. Challenge yourself to leave your comfort zone and pick a random subject. Try different genre styles. You never know what hidden songwriting talent you may unlock by giving it a try.

For example, you could choose something to write about from this list: a song for your grandma, sister, father, mother, brother, etc. (family is a great source of inspiration); a song for your significant other; a song about fishing; a song about a place that you have been; a song about a place in your imagination like a mountain, a beach, a small farm town, a long road trip, etc.

You can also pick a broader topic by exploring different genres, styles, or emotions. These are somewhat vague and can challenge you to feel your way into a mood.

Try writing a funny song... a blues, country, reggae, rock, ballad/love, spiritual, political, Christmas, holiday, environmental, happy, sad, or children's song... Try everything. You'll never know what you're really good at until you do.

"For me, songwriting is something I have to do ritually.
I don't just wait for inspiration;
I try to write a little bit every day."
—Sean Lennon

I wrote a song called "Burnt Bridges." Can you guess what that might be about?

Are you good at telling stories? That can be a very expressive way to write a song. How many famous songs can you think of that tell a story? I'm sure you can name a few. Do you have some stories to tell? Try to do it in a song...

Just get started. All you have to do is write some words and make some chord charts. Don't put pressure on yourself to write a hit every time you sit down to work on your songwriting. It's all about doing something and being proactive by trying to write.

"*I have a structured songwriting process. I start with the music and try to come up with musical ideas, then the melody, then the hook, and the lyrics come last.*"
—John Legend

I wrote a song I called "Thankful." It was a list of things that I am thankful for. I was working on a batch of songs at the time and I was also reading several books about the law of attraction. I never know where I will find inspiration. Something I read about expressing gratitude really struck a chord with me. I started thinking of things in my life that I was grateful for. It changed a little as it morphed into a song, and grateful became thankful. I have always been proud of this song and it makes me feel good whenever I perform it.

Another song I wrote, called "Ghost Train," is kind of a spiritual blues song about living in sin and knowing that the end is coming. This song took shape very quickly and was written to completion in one sitting. I was trying to strip down my guitar playing to a very basic rhythm and create a percussive vibe. It didn't take long for me to feel like I was thumping along like a train, and part of the inspiration in the lyrics came from the music I was making. The next thing I knew, I was singing words and it all flowed together really quickly. That doesn't happen to me all the time, and I was pretty happy with the song when I was done. I still play it the same way today.

I started to attempt to write a kids' album. The first and only song I wrote for it is called "Chasing Butterflies." I started thinking about two kids, a boy and a girl, holding hands in a field of grass and flowers while they chased after butterflies. I was writing the words and experimenting with the music and chords. Then I realized that the song was actually about two adults who were falling out of love. The image in my mind was of both of them leaving work early to go to the park, hold hands, and chase butterflies until they fell down laughing and were feeling happy together. Hopefully they would rekindle the "butterflies in the stomach" feeling they felt when they first met long ago. It stirs up fun imagery in my mind when I sing this song.

One of my most popular songs started by writing down words that a friend was saying. I saw a chance and grabbed my clipboard. Not every word in the song came out of her mouth, and not every word she said is in the song, but boy did it get me inspired. A few days later I shared the song with her and it was a very emotional moment to say the least. This song is called "Angels," and it always seems to touch people. I think there is some kind of universal appeal to the lyrics as well as the mood.

"Ain't You" is a song that is hard to explain. It's meant to be ambiguous so that anyone can relate to the concept. I could say I wrote it for a girl, or my guitar, or god, or whatever I was focused on at the time. It's just a basic song that conveys a mood through music and words.

For years, my favorite extended live version came in the form of my song "Even." I created a longer half-time intro for it to develop a dynamic buildup, and I really enjoyed presenting it in a live setting. It's a song about being in an unbalanced relationship and wanting it to even out somehow.

Another song that I worked up an extended live arrangement of is "Wall." This song is about the cliché of getting knocked down and getting back up again as life deals you obstacles to overcome, like a wall. It's about making changes and growing in order to get over the wall. Metaphors and analogies are great songwriting tools to make a point or explain a point of view that someone who has a different perspective can relate to.

I did write a song for my grandma called "Gram." She was very important to me. I spent a lot of time with her when I was younger and learned quite a bit about life, spending time in the kitchen watching her cook and listening to her talk. She had a lot of wisdom to share.

Sitting in the marina of a little beach town here in Florida I had the inspiration to write my song "The Storm." As you can imagine, it evokes the imagery of a storm, boats, and the water. I really tried to create a picture through the lyrical content. I also think the dynamic buildup helps give the feel of a storm rising to a climax.

My song "Ray" is a basic song about positive spiritual energy. The lyrics talk about trying to do the right thing and growing into a better version of myself. I would encourage everyone to try to write a song about some kind of personal growth. It is very rewarding.

I remember skipping school and going to a park with another guitar-playing friend of mine once when I was fifteen years old. I wrote a song that day called "Laughter and Tears." I am still drawn to this song, all these years later. I love a good ballad. I also tried to write what I thought was a country ballad. "Lil Lady" is the song that came from that idea. I have always thought that it would sound great with a piano part.

One year in the late nineties I was on the Oregon coast and went for a hike on the beach with some friends. We ended up climbing out onto some lava rocks and were mesmerized by our surroundings. We were so focused on what was going on in front of us that we didn't notice the rising tide starting to cover the beach that was our path back to safety. We had to climb higher on the rocks and struggled to make it back to the trail. I even lost a flip-flop because we were in a hurry, and the rocks cut it right off my foot. "Newport Beach to Salem" was the song I wrote about that experience.

"It's very helpful to start with something that's true. If you start with something that's false, you're always covering your tracks."
—Paul Simon

"Forgive Me" is a song I wrote in my early twenties that was inspired by the ninth of the twelve steps of recovery. I was hanging out with friends who were attending Alcoholics and Narcotics Anonymous meetings. I found a source of inspiration and wrote what I think is a pretty good song. I never know when inspiration will find me so I try to be aware.

I have written many songs over the years and each has its own unique meaning for me. I know some of my fans, friends, and family have their own favorites as well. I am sure they feel my passion in the performance and relate to the words I sing in each of their own individual ways. I strive to write from a perspective that will engage an audience that is full of diversity. I feel a lot of energy when I am inspired to write, and I really try to put it into my music.

 # MERCHANDISE AND TIP CAN

---

*"What differentiates sellers today is their ability
to bring fresh ideas."*
—Jill Konrath

Bring your own merchandise table and tip can! Do not use a bar stool or beer bucket. I consider it unprofessional and tacky. One bar stool can bring in $10,000 a year in revenue for the venue, so don't occupy one with your tip can. Hopefully a paying customer will sit on that stool, watch your show, like the music, and tip you. It doesn't matter how busy the bar is when you get there. The bar stool may be empty as you are setting up, but by the middle of your performance we will all hope that there isn't a single bar stool open.

I have a display with a tip can so people can buy my merchandise while I am playing a song.

I used to have a nice big glass tip jar. A drunk patron knocked it off the table many years ago and smashed it into a hundred pieces. I replaced it with a coffee can and it has stood the test of time. I have seen many types of tip cans over the years and it is definitely smart to try to draw attention to it. I like to make sure people can see my tip can so I keep it in front of me and highly visible. Hopefully, people will see it and drop some money in.

I usually take the money out of my tip can and stuff it into my pocket when I go on break. I do this because one year I was playing a gig on Thanksgiving and someone stole my tip money. Unfortunately, this happened... but I learned from the experience. My tip can money is quite often how I pay for gas and buy my lunch the next day.

I have played several places that just seem notorious for non-tipping audiences. One place I still play is like that. I was there last month and pulled a donut... zero tips! The previous two times I was there, I made five and twelve bucks. But at the gig right before that one, I had $148 in my tip can! It was a very rare occurrence in a venue I consider a dead zone for tips. Anything can happen, so we have to go with the flow and adapt to a different set of circumstances every single gig/show/night.

I will often put a can of bug spray by my tip can when I am playing an outdoor gig. Then I will make sure to announce that if anyone needs to use it, to feel free. I am not charging anyone to use the spray, but they usually throw a couple of bucks in my tip can.

BE CREATIVE WITH YOUR MERCH

I was once in a band that had a few fun items in our merch selection. Of course, the old standbys were there: CDs, stickers, and T-shirts. But we took it up a notch by offering koozies, lighters, and condoms. All of these items had our logo on them or on the packaging. Try to have fun with your merchandise items and if you can find something unique that matches your personality or creative energy, that's a great way to help you stand out and be remembered.

Why not sell (or even give away) balloons so the crowd can blow them up and bounce them around? I have considered offering beach balls as a merch item. I live at the beach and play many tiki bars and poolside shows, so I think it would be a lot of fun to see kids bouncing beach balls around.

The way I handle merchandise now is to have a display next to my tip can that advertises my items, as well as ways for people to give me tips. I used to keep a cardboard CD holder with a price sign on it and hoped that people would buy them by handing me the money or putting it into my tip can. This system worked well enough, but it also had its flaws. People were stealing my CDs. So now I keep my CDs and other merch items behind me on stage, in a case or a small box. I have four CDs and an eco-friendly guitar pick that I advertise for sale at my shows. My sign advertises for me and people can ask me for the items they want.

My merchandise sign also tells people how they can tip me. Of course, cash is still king, but there are newer ways to accept tips through apps. I advertise my Venmo and PayPal accounts so that people who do not have cash in their pocket will have the option of showing their appreciation for my music by sending me a tip from their phone. This is still new to me but it is working. At a gig just last week, I overheard a woman say she wished she had some cash so she could tip me. I just smiled and pointed at the sign next to my tip can and said, "Check it out." Presto—she tipped me $5 through Venmo. I have even seen some Solo Acoustic Musicians soliciting tips on their live Facebook video feeds. Your audience online can request a song and tip you money through a PayPal account.

People can also purchase my music on iTunes; on my website, they can click on a CD cover and be directly linked to my iTunes page. I even have the Square for my phone and my iPad, should someone choose to buy CDs from me at a show with a credit card. My CDs are completely solo acoustic music, just me and my guitar, not a full band.

PRIVATE PARTIES AND WEDDINGS

Most of the time it is just protocol to not put out merch or a tip can at private parties or wedding events. The client will often pay you a little extra to adjust for not having a tip can out, or will tip you a little extra at the end of the event. It's also worth remembering that these types of gigs pay a little better than a show at a bar, so the client not tipping is part of the territory and completely appropriate. When people have money to throw a private party for their friends, employees, etc., they do not want the musicians to solicit extra tips from their guests. Although we are always allowed to accept tips, some gigs do not want performers to ask for them in any way, even through merchandise setups.

TIP CAN FOR CHARITY

I was a Rotarian for four years and right off the bat, I saw an opportunity to use my skills with the guitar and singing to help others. Rotarian is the name for a member of a Rotary Club. Rotary Clubs are all over the US and the world, and are a positive force for community service. Whether in the form of actual physical endeavors to help people or a fundraiser of some kind, they are there to do good in the local community. Rotary International also strives to help people on a global level and has several different projects or funds for people to donate money to.

I decided I would give a small percentage of my tip can money to the Polio Plus Fund, which helps raise awareness and fight polio until it has been eradicated from the planet. In eight months I raised just over one thousand dollars with only a small portion of my tips. I gave it to the Rotary Foundation and received an award known as a Paul Harris Fellow. About a year later I reached Paul Harris Fellow Level Two, after another one-thousand-plus dollars of giving.

A few things happened while I was giving money to charity. One was that I noticed I was making a little more in tips. Another thing that happened was that word was spreading through the Rotary Clubs about what I was doing, so when I would meet Rotarians from other clubs, some of them would know a little bit about what I was up to.

The most memorable example of being recognized by a Rotarian from another club for what I had quickly achieved using my tip money came while I was at a city council meeting in my town. I was there with another member to accept a certificate from the city for a cleanup project we had spearheaded and completed. When we arrived, we were greeting other people in the room and I was introduced to the CEO of the local credit union. He said, "Wait a minute, are you the guy with the tip can? That is awesome work that you are doing!" I didn't know him or that he was in another local Rotary club. But he had heard of me and what I was accomplishing.

Of course, another major part of it was that I felt good about what I was doing. I had a sense of accomplishment because I set a goal, worked towards it, and achieved it. I will continue to find ways to use my skill set to help others and give back to the community.

About five years ago, I was on a gig in a nice little town in the Tampa Bay area called Safety Harbor and had a great night with my tip can. The city blocks off the street for a monthly event called "Third Friday." I was playing a local restaurant and bar on Main Street, right in the middle of all the festivities. It was a three-hour gig, from 8-11 PM, that paid $150. I was really engaging the crowd and sharing a lot of positive energy. The people were giving that energy back and I did not take a break for the whole three hours.

With so many other things going on around us, and lots of other choices of things to do right outside the door, I did not want to lose half the crowd by taking fifteen to twenty minutes off, so I just kept playing. By the end of the night I had sold eight CDs at $10 apiece and had pulled in $186 my tip can. I went to the owner and told him that he now owed me $36 to match the tips that the people had paid me. I asked him to match the tip amount because it was more than he was paying me. I also made sure he knew that I did not take a break at all and really tried to keep the place jam-packed with people. He agreed with my logic and added $36 to my pay for a $186 total.

That was a pretty good night for a Solo Acoustic Musician, as far as I am concerned. I made $452 on a three-hour gig five minutes from my house. ($150 pay + $186 tips + $80 cd sales + $36 tip match = $452 total)

This was a rare occurrence and I have grown to never expect or count on anything like it. This helps me feel really grateful when something like that does happen. It is truly a blessing when the people in the crowd show their appreciation for what you are doing by clapping and tipping you well. I consider it a successful tip can night any time I make more than $20. It can start to feel normal to make $20 to $30 in tips, so it always sticks out as a great night when I make $50, $70, or over $100 on a gig.

Even though CDs are becoming less and less relevant, they can still be used as a reason to throw a party and promote our newest recordings. In the past, I would purchase a thousand CDs at a time through DiscMakers. Now, I would suggest a smaller batch of a hundred CDs. You can pre-autograph the CDs and make them a collector's item. Let people know there are only a hundred units available so they know that the CDs are special. It's also possible to go out with download cards and flash drives these days.

At my last CD release party I gave away a can of beer with each purchase. I threw my party at a bar I had been playing music in for years. I knew the owners well and they worked with me on my event. I also asked a local brewery to donate a couple of cases of beer. So I had forty-eight cans of beer to give away to people who bought a CD. It was fun to be able to add that giveaway to all of my promotions for the party.

Only do one release party per CD, and try to make it a special event about your music. I did ask a couple of other local SAMs to be opening acts. I included their names on all my promotional materials and each of them played a half-hour set of original music before I went on. I played all twelve songs from my new CD and a couple of my older songs. My set lasted just under an hour. By the end of the night I had sold almost one hundred CDs. I was very happy with the outcome and grateful for all my friends who came out to support my music that evening.

NETWORKING WITH OTHER MUSICIANS

"We are at a crossroads in the music business: with the rise of the internet, the world we live in has changed, and the past is not coming back. But I see the glass as half-full: the internet and social networking are new avenues for the next Bob Dylan to be born on."
—Jon Bon Jovi

Building a network with other musicians is really important to making this "gigging for a living" thing into a reality. Other musicians can help cover each other's shifts, help each other get into new venues that have just opened up, and share a wealth of local knowledge about what's going on around town. There are times when a manager, owner, or agent will mistreat another one of your Solo Acoustic Musician peers and it can come in really handy to be privy to that kind of information. New places are opening up all the time and as a group, local musicians can provide many referrals for other musicians to get work.

One way to build longevity on your local scene is to make friends and network with some of the other musicians. You may not get along with all the other players on your scene, but I am sure you will find some friends and lots of people in the community who will be willing to help each other. Try going to open mics to meet other fellow musicians and songwriters. Most are based on a singer-songwriter format and are a haven for Solo Acoustic Musicians. There are also open jam sessions out there, which is a different type of format. The room will still have other local musicians to meet, but they will be involved in a full-band jam-out situation, playing together.

I would also like to encourage you to go out on your nights off and watch other SAMs do their thing. I have seen most of my counterparts on the local scene in my area play at least one set of a gig and when I hear of a new name I don't know, I will try to go somewhere they are playing to check them out. I find it a great way to actually meet them and see what they do in person. Most of them have video online that I can watch but I like to actually be on site and get a feel for what they are doing. This knowledge of what they do and how they act on the gig can help me determine whether I would ask them to cover for me. Anytime I go out of town or get sick, for example, I will probably be going down a list of fellow Solo Acoustic Musicians to find someone who can fill in for me and do a good job.

HOST AN OPEN MIC

A great way to become part of a network of musicians is to attend or host an open mic night. Hosting an open mic can also be a way to make money on an off night, as most are held on weeknights. Weekends are usually busier in the bars, and therefore those nights do not need the extra promotion that goes into making an open mic work. This can help you in the pursuit of vertical employment. As a host of the open mic you can build a core group of musicians who will come out on a regular basis, allowing you to meet and network with them. We can all learn a lot from each other and hopefully make some friends along the way.

When moving to a new town, if you have the gear and the ability to run an open mic, then you can at least fill an "off night" weekly spot on your calendar by hosting one. What I mean by "off night" is a non-weekend night. For example, you could be the host of an open mic every Monday night at a local bar, brewery, or restaurant. I moved to Florida in 2008 and started an open mic that ran for years. I still know musicians from that experience. Some of them are local and some of them are seasonal "snowbirds" who come down to Florida every year from somewhere cold up north. In many ways, running an open mic is like a regular gig, except you are sharing stage time, running sound, and accommodating the other musicians' needs. So the extra cable, microphone, mic stand, and accessories we addressed in an earlier chapter will come in handy.

In order to host a successful open mic night, you have to promote it. There are many ways to do this, and of course social media is a very important tool for that these days. I have always tried to get the venue to help me with promotion. This didn't always work. But the owners and managers that did help me promote open mics always saw increased attendance.

Old-school tactics still work. Do not underestimate the power of a physical flyer in the venue where you are hosting your open mic. Hopefully the establishment has a customer base who will see it and spread the word. You should also put flyers on the pushpin boards at all local music stores. You never know where you might find your next steady repeat performer.

Try to remember to ask each new person who comes to the open mic where they heard about it and why they are there. Maybe they are visiting, or are new to town, or trying to make friends to start a band. As a host, over time you will get to know a lot of musicians in your area and you might be able to point them in the right direction to meet people who share their musical interests.

SOCIAL MEDIA GROUPS

Another way to network with other musicians is on Facebook through joining or creating groups. These groups can help you find gigs, find duo partners, find places to play, find coverage for when you are sick or planning a trip out of town, and also help you to just make friends. I am a member of a couple of groups like these that consist of other musicians who help each other out. Members post every day with availability or a need for coverage. Groups like these can create a sense of community that can even reach past your local area and help you grow your network regionally.

There are also Facebook groups for posting open mic flyers. I don't host an open mic anymore but I still see other friends' posts and updates to these groups, so I know where and when quite a few open mics are being held. Every now and then I pop in and hang out. I like to listen to other musicians, especially if they are playing original songs. Sometimes I still get messages asking me when and where to go for an open mic, and I direct people to those pages.

I have been known to help musicians who are new in town, or people who are just starting to play out live, getting them into places and getting them a foot in the door on my recommendation. I do not see any of them as competition because I have confidence that I am good at what I do and that I provide quality music for my clients. I even have clients asking me to send them a few new musicians, and I will absolutely help them to find new talent. More often than not, my relationship with the client grows stronger after I help them to hire another good musician.

I was approached recently by a waiter at one of my steady gigs and asked if I could help him get some gigs. He had just started playing out live. He said that his earliest gigs went very well, and one place in particular definitely wanted to hire him to play more shows. I gave him my card and told him to email me some video footage so I could see what kind of stuff he was doing. I said I was confident that I could help him get into a few new places if I thought he would be a good fit for them. I know quite a few owners and managers who respect my referrals enough to get him a gig.

I really do enjoy seeing my other musician friends succeed, whether that means they are staying busy and playing good gigs or maybe they have finally put out the CD they have been working on for the last year. I try to congratulate the friends I have made for any milestones that they achieve. A part of being in the community and sharing the common bond of being a Solo Acoustic Musician is the mutual experience that we all go through. One big life change is quitting your day job and becoming a full-time working musician. Some people can't believe that it is possible to do, but it is.

*"Music is one of the most powerful things the
world has to offer. No matter what race or religion
or nationality or sexual orientation or gender
that you are, it has the power to unite us."*
—Lady Gaga

Whether it was a good gig or bad gig, we can all bond over stories about what happened out there on the scene. I see this kind of interaction in local musician groups on Facebook all the time. Someone will post something about a really good gig and how they were treated with respect or got an unusually generous tip, and the rest of the group will chime in with comments of support or similar experiences. Then someone will post about how the worst heckler they have ever encountered was at their gig earlier and was so obnoxious that they didn't know how to handle it. Of course, people in the group will once again chime in with support and then usually a barrage of comments will flow in that describe funny comebacks and witty banter to use on hecklers in the future. So while we are alone on the stage at the gig, we are not the only ones out there going through these things.

LUTHIERS

There are usually a small group of guys in any given area who are luthiers. These are the people who can fix your guitar and provide maintenance as well. It's like taking my guitar to the doctor for a checkup. I recently had new frets installed on my Martin guitar. I will be replacing the bridge and saddle soon as well. About once a year I will get my neck adjusted and have a basic setup done. This helps my guitar stay in good shape and ready to play. When the wear and tear caused by playing a lot and the constant humidity set in, it can cause fret buzz and make it a struggle to stay in tune. It's also nice to know these people in case a bigger problem arises. In the past year I have had two giant cracks appear in the body of my Martin. Thankfully I knew the guys to call and was able to get my guitar into the shop for a quick repair.

Be on the scene, be a part of the scene, get out there and meet other musicians who are doing the same thing.

 **PROMOTION**

Without promotion, something
terrible happens... nothing!
—P.T. Barnum

The point of promotion is to make people aware of your musical projects and to get them to come to your shows. I want people to check out my website and buy my original music on iTunes. I also want people to come see me play live. This, like booking, is part of the office-type work I must do to make my full-time musician lifestyle a success. I try to be creative in how I share my music and my schedule with friends and fans. There are many ways to promote yourself and to let people know what you are up to.

In my mind, promoting gigs is a shared responsibility between the venue and myself. I will do my part to get the word out to my friends and fans about when and where I am playing. I expect the places I play to do the same thing by spreading the word about live music in their location and advertising the musicians on their roster. Each place handles promotion differently, so when I am booking with a new venue, I will bring this topic up in conversation as early as possible.

I still do several things in an old-school way, and promotion is one of them. I will often call friends to let them know about some upcoming shows. This is a very personal way to invite people, and it will mean a lot more to them, which increases the odds of them coming to a show. I find this to be particularly true if I am trying to sell tickets or being paid a share of the door. A similar promo tactic is the small group text message. Again, it is more personal than a poster or a social media post, but can include a couple dozen friends at a time. It is also helpful if I am resting my voice and want to avoid a lot of talking on the phone.

Keeping an updated calendar and directing people to my website is another way to promote my gigs. I hand out a lot of business cards with my website on them and tell people to find me online or email me for my schedule. It can be a lot like office work, but it is part of the job to add dates and times on a constant basis. Some SAMs put out a weekly or a monthly post on social media listing their upcoming shows. When it comes to your website, I would suggest adding dates as soon as you book them for at least a couple of months out. And don't forget to make changes if there are mix-ups or cancellations!

I am lucky enough to play many places that do not require or need my promotion because they already have a thriving business with many regular customers. I can make a choice to tell friends or make online flyers to let people know where I am, but these places do not pressure me to bring anyone or to build a following in their locations. Where I live, many people come to our area seasonally, which always boosts the number of customers frequenting the local establishments. I grew up in a resort beach town and have lived in big cities too. I find it only helps me to live in an area of high population density. There are a lot of places to play and a lot of people to meet. I have fans in a lot of different towns in the Tampa Bay area and they will come see me when I am in their part of the bay.

POSTERS

I have a very dear friend who is a graphic artist and she has helped me many times by designing quality posters for online and print. She has also designed CD covers for me, among other things, and I am very grateful to be blessed by her friendship and her talents. I will send her a picture and we will then talk about the information I want to include on the posters. When the design is done I will print them out. There are a couple of ways I put the flyers up.

I have also commissioned artists to make art for me in the past. I am not afraid to pay someone for their talent and time in order to get a good poster or some artwork for my promotional materials. It is also a good way to make you more a part of the artistic community. Graphic artists charge for their services, as they should, but they are worth it.

A standard 8.5" x 11" piece of paper can work for very small establishments that I play, but for larger venues I will print out an 11" x 17" poster. I am sure you have all seen posters like this where the date and time is written with marker in the open space at the bottom of the poster. I have a few places that I play once a month and what I do for them is something I find unique. I will print out two posters and laminate them together back-to-back. When I place these posters in a window, people will be able to read them from both sides, and I can update my dates and times at the bottom with a dry erase marker. When I arrive to play, I change the date and time to my next scheduled appearance.

I don't like to litter the bar and the tables with little flyers, but some places like that. In this case it is best to get your art to fit into four sections of a standard piece of paper. You will be able to cut every page you print into quarters, and have four separate small flyers to place in the venue. I have employed this technique when I was running an open mic in the past. This is also good for placing flyers in music stores to let other musicians know about when and where an open mic is going to be happening. Leaving a small stack next to the pushpin board will encourage people to take one.

If you can afford it, a professional photographer can really help you with promotions. A legit photo shoot of you with your guitar can take your graphics to another level. When I am making a poster or a CD cover, I will reach out to my network of friends and other musicians to get referrals for good photographers. Remember, you may be able to trade for a photo shoot. I was approached by a photographer who wanted to use my song "Angels" on her website. Her web designer and lawyer told her that she needed my permission, and we struck a deal: she could use my song on her website if she would do a photo shoot for me. This worked out great for both of us.

SOCIAL MEDIA

I stick to the basics and pretty much only use Facebook. I can post about where and when I am playing by simply typing in the information or uploading an image of a flyer. I can also make events and invite people from my friends list. When I announce an event, I will encourage the venue's owner or manager to promote it as well, making them a co-host or sending them links they can share with their friends and fans.

Facebook Live has become a new way to promote your talents. People can see you on a gig from wherever they are. I am not on Instagram or Twitter, but these are also current ways to promote yourself. Our technology is constantly evolving and as a Solo Acoustic Musician, you have to make use of what's available and what works for you. I am sure that every year a couple of new sites or apps will appear and become useful marketing and promotional tools for all musicians.

RADIO

In the past I have made a few appearances on local radio stations that do a really good job of working with local musicians to promote their original music. You can find two of these appearances on my website. Something that I did and I would suggest that you do is write down the topics that you want to discuss during your interview. Lay out the songs that you want to play as well. I actually prepared more subjects than necessary to talk about, just to cover my bases. The shows I appeared on were one hour long, and I wanted to have some control over where the conversation would go, so that the host did not ask me questions about things I didn't want to talk about. I was able to maximize promotion by pointing out the places and websites I wanted people to hear about.

One of my radio appearances actually helped me land a very well-paying gig at a popular festival on the beach. The day after I was on, I was approached by a man who worked for the city of Treasure Island, Florida. He complimented me on my music and told me he thought I was funny on the show the night before. He then asked me if I was available to play music at their annual sand sculpture event. Artists from around the country and even a few from Europe come to Treasure Island, FL, every year and make sculptures with the beach sand. I was surprised, and was honored to accept the invitation. I was actually already booked that night, but he wanted me for a two-hour slot in the afternoon, so it worked out for both of us. I picked up a good gig and made a new contact by doing radio promotion.

In the end, all of this is helping me create and identify my own brand. Just like booking, promotion is about sales. I want to sell CDs, downloads, tickets, and any other merchandise I might have as a Solo Acoustic Musician. Promotion can also be used as leverage when negotiating fees. If you can show a professional level of marketing to a business or client that you are trying to book a gig with, you might be able to get more money out of the deal.

 **BOOKING**

"Our greatest weakness lies in giving up. The most certain way to succeed is always to try just one more time."
—Thomas Edison

While this is the "office work" part of the job, you can still be creative with parts of it, and stand out from the many, many other musicians trying to get gigs.

I used to know a drummer who booked his band. He would find out things about the person in charge of booking at the venue and send creative packages to them. One of these packages included a box of the manager's favorite cereal along with a cover letter and demo CD. (This was several years ago, when CD demos were mailed in manila envelopes, along with press clippings, song lists, and anything else you thought might help you get a gig.) These days, one of the first steps in booking a show is to make a promo video that you can email, text, and share with potential clients through social media direct messages. I am saving a lot of money on postage by not having to send out hundreds of packages anymore.

Every place you are going to deal with will have their own way of doing things. Some managers or owners prefer to do all their booking only between nine and ten AM on Tuesday mornings. That is a very specific example I have encountered. Some people will prefer to talk about booking by phone, while others will prefer text messages. Some like to use email and some will want you to message them on social media. We SAMs have to adapt to a lot of situations and each client's ways of doing things.

I believe that the original way to book a gig is just as good now as it was back then, and that is to actually go to the bar or restaurant and make your sales pitch to the entertainment director. Every now and then, it's good for me to just hop in the van and go for a drive, stopping at different establishments along the way. Some managers and owners will be there and I will chat with them about booking. Others will not, and I will leave my card, taking their card with me so I can follow up about working together. This is an old-school, face-to-face technique that I still think is highly effective.

Make a unique business card that will stand out from the others. I have a very good friend who does graphic design for me. I am blessed every time she works on a project for me. My card has a picture of me on the front, and a QR code on the back that directs people to my website.

WEBSITE VS. EPK (ELECTRONIC PRESS KIT)

These are essentially the same thing, and both of them can help you book gigs. You should have one or the other, so you can send a link to potential clients. If you want to use both of them, then go for it. A promo video may get a much quicker response than a whole website or EPK, so making one of those is a good idea. Placing your promo video on your homepage is another valuable strategy. You can also share your promo video through all of your social media outlets. My website is michaelnicholsmusic.com, and the SAM website is soloacousticmusician.com.

WHAT DO I CHARGE FOR A GIG?

Several factors are involved in quoting a price to a potential client: the amount of time you are going to play, the place or event you are playing, the type of gig it is, etc. A gig fee equation might start with a base rate of $50 per hour, making a three-hour gig $150 and a four-hour gig $200. Now, I have had the good fortune to make much more than that on special occasions. But this is a decent minimum guideline for working a bar or restaurant gig. Mind you, every place is different and will have different budgets or pay scales. I have to make the decision whether or not I want to take a gig based on the amount of time they want me to play and the pay they are offering. Sometimes when I quote a price they think is too high, they will just end communication. It can be a little bit of a tricky dance, and I deal with all sorts of personalities in this business. Negotiating is almost always a challenge, but I stand firm. I believe I am offering a quality product and service that deserves to be paid for accordingly.

I used to have a Wednesday evening gig that lasted three hours—from five to eight PM—and paid $250 plus tips and a meal. The venue was a rather large and high-end beach resort hotel with what I would consider a large budget. They paid me better than average for the town I was working in, and I did not expect to get that same pay scale at every other place I was playing. I knew that I could not charge my other clients that same rate because it would be outside their budget.

I always ask to include some form of food and beverage allowance or tab as part of my compensation. Every place has a different policy, though, so while one place gives you free everything, another may allot you a $25 tab to use at your discretion for food or beverage. Other places may offer you half-price food but no help on alcoholic beverages. It is standard practice that musicians do not pay for non-alcoholic beverages, period. You are working and need access to water, tea, coffee, or soda.

VERTICAL EMPLOYMENT

When you look at your calendar and can book a regular Monday gig, for example, you are filling your schedule with what I call vertical employment. I had Monday, Tuesday, and Wednesday night gigs at the same three places for almost four years. This is a hard thing to pull off for so long, but it was great while it lasted. Unfortunately, I lost all three gigs in a period of two months. I learned from that to try and pair up bi-weekly gigs at multiple places. This way if I lose one or two of those, I will still have the others until I replace what has been lost. I am currently working a seven-to-ten PM shift every other Sunday on the beach, two alternating Monday and Tuesday gigs in town, and one every other Wednesday. This affords me a certain amount of stability and freedom to make plans and choices for the weekends.

The rest of my calendar is a constant blend of existing and new clients. Fridays and Saturdays are the easiest days of the week to find gigs, so I usually don't choose to apply the vertical employment method to those days of the week. If you want to play the same place every Friday night and that works for you, then do it. It's just not for me. Venues have rotation systems, too, and each one will find the formula that works for them. Some places will book me for a year, some will book six months out, and some places seem to book the next month at the last minute. I have several places I play that book me once or twice a month, several that I play three times a year, and so on... this system keeps my calendar full and gets the bills paid.

OVERSATURATION

Playing in the same town five nights a week can be a challenge. It will become hard to keep it fresh for yourself and the regulars when you play the same places with this much regularity. I like to find one spot to play regularly in each little town near me. This way I make local fans all over my home area without burning myself out in just one part of town.

I guess how you will work this out depends on where you live. I try to keep most of my jobs within an hour's drive of my home. There are some exceptions. I live in a densely populated area that supports many smaller cities in the four counties that make up the Tampa Bay area. When I used to live in Baltimore, Maryland, the city was surrounded by a beltway and all of the different suburbs that came with it. I even went forty-five minutes down the road to Annapolis every Tuesday for a steady gig that lasted for years.

BALANCE

Booking takes up a lot of our free time when we choose to live this life. It's very important to try to find balance within your schedule so you can do the things you want to do. Trying to keep a calendar full and also find time for healthy activities can be a challenge.

I keep it simple. Sometimes I just disengage from the computer, email, or whatever else I am doing for booking and take a break. For me this includes not multitasking while making my lunch. Rather, I will spend my time enjoying the event of lunch itself. Whether I am going to stay home and make my own lunch or go down the street to the diner, I consciously choose to use this time to relax. I often find myself by the pool or at the beach for thirty to ninety minutes, weather permitting. I read, work in the garden, meditate, or just relax and enjoy being outside.

It may seem a little bit silly to preach about getting outside and doing something, but it helps me recharge and give off positive energy when I'm on stage. Everyone will have a different life balance to find for themselves. I'm just telling you that it's very important. Even if you are not on a big stage in front of thousands of people, it is still important to have some positive energy to give to the people who are there. Usually, after being outside for a little while, when I decide to check my emails again, I will see responses to emails, texts, and social media messages that I sent out. This is how I find balance and quit spending too much time on the computer. Speaking of which, it's time for a break from typing... so I'm going out to the pool with a cup of sweet tea and a good book... I'll be back later!

BOOKING ORIGINAL MUSIC

I can, and do, play original songs at my regular cover-song gigs. I believe that it is my choice if I want to add an original song into my set list. But part of making a living by playing my guitar and singing is booking gigs where I am encouraged to play my original songs and sell my CDs. If you don't have enough original songs to play a few hours (with breaks), you can also book a gig for you and two or three other songwriters. This is a great way to land a paying original gig and get to play a show with some other local musicians and thereby build your friendship network.

Breweries can be a great place to play original music. I think that there is a correlation between craft beer and the homemade "crafting" of songs. Some people make beer and some people make music, and there is often a feeling of mutual appreciation for people who make things and share them with their friends. I play a brewery in Lakeland, Florida, about an hour away from my home, that has a local market event on certain weekends. It's fun when I play there to walk around and check out what all the vendors are selling, and there is a local brewing club giving out samples of their home brews.

DO YOU HAVE A DRAW?

I try my best to provide quality music for the people in the audience in front of me. Remember, as a Solo Acoustic Musician, you should not be expected to "draw" a crowd at all. That is what popular bands do! Not Solo Acoustic Musicians— our job is to entertain or play songs in the background for the patrons of the establishment that hired us. If a bar, restaurant, brewery, or some other kind of place that is hiring musicians asks if you have a draw, you should be honest with them. I am one person and not a four- or five-piece band with a huge following.

I was once asked by a bar owner how many friends I had on Facebook. I answered him and he told me that I should be able to bring at least fifty people every time I play a gig. This is what I consider to be an example of exaggerated expectations. I actually did book some gigs with him for a string of Tuesday night performances for about four months out. The first time I played there I brought in thirty-three friends. (Yes, I counted!) The owner was impressed and happy that night. Unfortunately, he expected me to bring in more people every week, and the reality was that every week fewer and fewer of my friends were coming to this bar.

About six weeks into the booking, he confronted me about not bringing in more people and I explained to him that most of my friends who came out during the first few weeks were not going to be coming back to see me play at his bar anymore. They were all telling me that the service was nonexistent, the food was slow to be brought out, and they were being served cold flat bread pizzas. There were even complaints that the bartender was ignoring them while he talked to his friends, who he was comping free drinks at the other end of the bar. So, while I tried hard to get my fans and friends to come see me in his place, they were being chased away by his staff.

He refused to believe anything I was saying, and that working relationship ended abruptly.

TAXES AND AGENTS

While I do file taxes, and so should you, I am no expert at all in these areas. My suggestion for any working musician is to find a good accountant and make a plan for keeping track of your financial information.

While I do work with a few agents, I don't wish to offer too much advice in this area. I don't need to work with any of the agents I know in order to keep my calendar full. I have always been capable of booking my own gigs and making a living. So I never let any of them handle my calendar exclusively. This way if anything goes wrong in the arrangement, I will still have gigs on my calendar that I booked myself, and I won't lose out on too many shows. Agents can be tough to deal with, as most of the time they are not musicians or creative types at all, and they simply want to make as much money as they can.

It is very hard work keeping a calendar full and I have to deal with many different owners and managers, so when I do get an email or call from an agent about a gig, it can be a blessing. While dealing with agents can be stressful sometimes, it is also beneficial to me to supplement my calendar with the gigs they provide.

Knowing the difference between agents is important. A booking agent will try to sell you to many venues for a percentage of the booking fee. But a talent agent will work with many different venues and will usually charge each venue a fee to provide them with an act. What I call a third-party agent is one that will take over a venue's calendar and require artists to go through them to get booked there. This person is not an employee of the venue, hence the term "third-party." Sometimes this can even be another local musician that you know. I mostly work with the latter and only take two or three gigs from any kind of agent at one time.

Good luck in these areas.

THE GIVEAWAY

There is always an opportunity for you to use your skills and equipment to help other people. So when I am approached by someone who is involved with putting on a charity event, I always ask them, what is the cause or charity? The second question is always, when is the event? Several things can happen in this situation.

I can be available and provide them with live music at no charge. I can be booked already on a paying gig, and have to decline because I am committed somewhere else. Or I can have a gig later that day that pays me, and do their event for free earlier in the day. As I stay booked pretty steadily, the latter is usually what happens.

I donated my time for a community garden fundraiser event recently, and played a set for free. It was something that made me feel good; I was involved in my community, and helped raise money to further a quality local project. It was a multi-act concert with several other solo and duo performers. The event raised more than $3200 through donations, a 50/50 raffle, and a silent auction with prizes donated by local businesses. The bar where the event was held also chipped in by teaming up with a local brewery that donated a keg, and all sales of that beer were donated to the community garden organization.

I am contacted occasionally to play music for a celebration of life (a wake). It is obviously easier for me to say yes when it is not a weekend, because most of my Fridays and Saturdays are booked well in advance. A couple of years ago, I was contacted by a friend whom I had known for about ten years, asking me to play music on a Monday evening at a local restaurant. One of her good friends had passed on a few days earlier, and she wanted to get a bunch of his friends together to remember him. I didn't actually know the guy, but we had a lot of mutual friends and I had the evening off, so I donated my time free of charge. Every now and then she still thanks me for playing music that night.

On another occasion, I provided the PA system for several other musicians to play songs at a celebration of life. I did play a few songs myself, but I mostly just ran the sound for some of the other local musician friends of the family.

A few years ago I donated my time to DJ a fundraiser for a kids' charity that took place in a local park down the street. I was approached about a week beforehand by a friend whom I had known for several years through other mutual friends. She wanted me to play and sing. I was working about eight gigs that week and had a gig the same day, later in the evening. So I offered to bring my iPod and a small PA setup to provide music, and a microphone to make announcements. It was a fun two-hour event in the early afternoon. I went home and relaxed a little before heading out to my evening gig. It feels good to use my talent, or in this case my equipment, to help other people and be a part of my community.

I was once approached by a music teacher at the local middle school, who asked me to come in and do some live demonstrations during her classes. I set up in the front of the classroom with my guitar, amp, and pedals. As each class started, the teacher would introduce me and I would play guitar for a few minutes to grab their attention and get them interested in what I was doing. After that, I began to explain what I was doing and give a general presentation about guitar and making music. The next part of the demonstration was the question-and-answer section, and the kids had many questions. It was a lot of fun, and I hope that I inspired a few children in that classroom to pursue a musical instrument on some level. They don't all have to become full-time musicians for music to change their lives in a positive way.

THE BREAK EVEN

When I get paid just enough for a gig to match my expenses, it usually means I am doing it in order to justify travelling somewhere I want to go. Sometimes it can be beneficial to make such a trade-off in order to gain new experiences or see old friends and family.

I was hired to play a holiday party for an architecture firm located in the Washington, DC, area. My plane ticket to Baltimore was about $250. My PA rental from the local music store was $150. So my expenses were already totalling about $400. The blessing was that the gig I booked for this trip paid $750. The party was on the second floor of a very nice restaurant, so I had quite the load-in up the stairs. Everyone helped me on the load-out down the stairs at the end of the party. I was handed an envelope with cash and thanked for doing a great job. Then I had some extra cash and a few days with family in the area. All in all it was a pretty good break-even gig!

I made two trips up north in a single year that took me to Connecticut, Boston, and New York City. The gigs I was hired to play paid enough to cover my plane tickets and still have a little spending money left over. I was able to stay with some friends just outside of Hartford and they were also kind enough to transport me to the gigs. With their help, I was able to save on transportation and lodging. They even took me to a few wineries on the days between gigs. On another day off we were able to go up to Springfield, Massachusetts, and tour the Basketball Hall of Fame. One more day trip took us into Boston for the day before the gig that night. Hiking along the Freedom Trail and experiencing the city for the day was delightful. We had lunch in Little Italy and a shot of Jameson at the Black Rose bar.

Both trips were a lot of fun and I got to see many friends that lived up there. For me, though, the main highlight was opening for a band on a party boat that left Manhattan to go up the river to the Statue of Liberty. The boat pulled up really close to Ellis Island and everyone was able to take great pictures of the statue at night. It was a definite once-in-a-lifetime event for me and for my friends, who I was able to bring to the party. I doubt I will ever be that close to the Statue of Liberty again.

Side note... When playing on a boat, take a wide stance with your legs. I was almost thrown backwards into the drum set when the weather changed and the boat started to rock back and forth.

I recently booked a gig in St. Thomas that I am hoping to make into an annual event. The fee is really just enough for my plane ticket but I am also being housed in a very nice condo for a week. I am told the condo rents for over two thousand dollars for a week. I only play on two of the days: a three-hour show on Saturday afternoon and another on Sunday afternoon. I will be able to eat some meals for free at the bar I am playing. I have always wanted to go to St. Thomas, and now my guitar is helping me get there. I am sure I will build friendships and cultivate more contacts once I am on the island. I am looking forward to going on a fishing charter on one of my days off and relaxing on the beach for most of the time. I consider this a great trade-off and a definite example of the break-even!

Travel Tip: When I am travelling on a plane with my acoustic guitar, I will loosen my strings drastically or just take them off completely. The cabin is pressurized and safe for my acoustic guitar. When I gate check my acoustic guitar to the bottom of the plane, the environment is different. There is tension on tight strings and the pressure in the storage compartment. The temperature in the underbelly of the plane is also very cold. By removing the strings or loosening them a lot, I relieve the tension. If I don't do one of these two things, I run the risk of my guitar's neck breaking off the body. I make sure to bring extra strings and a Snark Tuner in my guitar case, so as soon as I get where I am going I can put on new strings and get tuned up.

THE TAKEAWAY

This is when you are fortunate enough to land a very well-paying gig and hopefully less time working.

In 2018, a hurricane was about to hit North Carolina and quite a few people were coming to Florida to get away from the storm. I was called to play a wedding cocktail hour at the last minute and was able to be there. I had a gig afterwards already booked and the timing of my transition between gigs worked out pretty smoothly. The bride and groom had some family in Tampa Bay and rerouted as many friends and relatives as they could to the area. On this gig I played music for one hour for a payment of $300... plus a $50 tip!

For three years in a row, I played a Fourth of July party for the same family. I consider their house to be like a mansion on the water. The parties had catering, a bartender, and even some game company rentals with prizes for high scores. Most of the prizes were $50 gift cards to places like Best Buy and

Amazon. Their neighborhood association even got a barge to park just offshore for a really good fireworks show. I would play a three-hour show with breaks and be paid $400. Then, they would actually tip me three $50 bills on top of my pay. Gigs like these are great to have!

Booking is about salesmanship. This means I have to constantly follow up with people to keep my calendar full. It even means I have to make sure to follow up with clients that I have been working with for a long time. Quite a few of my clients only book two to three months out, so we are in contact very often. I have been doing this a long time and I still have to sing for my supper too. I'm always in touch with new owners, new managers, and new venues because the music scene is constantly changing. So I always have to stay actively informed and up to date with the ever-changing landscape of my local scene.

Bars come and go all the time. Managers and employees come and go all the time. There have been times when it takes following up and meeting three different new general managers in a period of a few months, because the turnover rate for employees in bars is very high. I have seen a place close, only to have a new owner buy the location and want to have live music. It happens all the time and it is a challenge to keep up with the ever-changing gig environment. Sometimes there are locations that appear to be "dead" until the right owner takes over and makes the right changes. Then it becomes a successful spot with live music every night of the week. I am blessed to play a few places like what I just described.

One way to sell yourself is to pick dates you want and ask for them. I like certain holidays and sometimes they fall on weekdays, which can help me fill empty spots on my calendar. Some holidays will fall on your weekly vertical employment gigs. I have a standing gig every other Monday and I planned it ahead of time to line up with Memorial Day and Labor Day. This gives me a few extremely busy Mondays throughout the year. Another specific date that I will pitch to places is the night before Thanksgiving. That Wednesday is one of the biggest bar nights of the year, every year. Other holidays will migrate through the week as the years pass. The Fourth of July may be a Thursday this year, but last year it was probably on a Wednesday. Cinco De Mayo and St. Patrick's Day are also examples of big bar nights to sell yourself for.

Annual festivals or downtown events can work in a way similar to holidays. There is an annual blues festival near where I live, and the downtown area is blocked off for foot traffic only. About fifteen to twenty thousand people come out each year to hear the blues music all over town. Every bar or restaurant has a blues musician, and the city also provides a few stages with top-notch blues bands all day and evening. We also have seafood festivals, beer festivals, and other "concert in the park" series. I try to sell myself for any of these that I think my music would fit. As a Solo Acoustic Musician, I usually get an early afternoon opening spot because a larger headlining band will be on later. This works out great for me; I get to play in front of a large crowd, get paid, and still go play a nighttime gig somewhere else.

AUDITIONING

Before moving to Florida I never auditioned for gigs. I used to send a promo package with a song list, some press clippings, and a demo CD. The very first year I moved here, I hit the streets and visited as many bars as I could, looking for work. I was asked to come down and audition. I was reluctant because I had never been asked to do that before. But I went down to the bar, set up, and played some songs in the hopes of getting some gigs.

By the third song, the entertainment director came over and told me I could stop and that they wanted to hire me. She further informed me that all the managers of the bar, restaurant, and the hotel were sitting at the table with her and that all of them thought I was excellent, and that they would like to hire me for every Monday for the next year. This was an excellent opportunity for me, especially since I had just moved to a new city and state all the way down the East Coast from everything and everyone that I knew.

I can honestly say that it inspired me to initiate the audition process if I thought the booking conversations with some- one seemed to have stalled. I have booked a gig every single time I did an audition. I never play more than one hour for a free audition, and doing it has helped get me into new places that become clients for years to come. So yes, I believe in the audition. It is not the first thing I would do or suggest, but if I am struggling with getting communication from a manager at a place I want to play, then I can employ this option to try and open the line of communication back up, get on site with my gear, and show them what I can do.

I recently received an email about upcoming auditions for a very large hotel in downtown Tampa. I had been emailing their managers for about a year with no response so I was happy to finally have some correspondence. We set up a time and I drove down to audition. I arrived early and grabbed a glass of water at the bar. I asked for the manager contact from my email and waited. The bartender told me they were having some other auditions and that the manager would be with me in a bit.

At the scheduled time, I was approached by yet another manager and escorted to a ballroom on the second floor. This was not what I was expecting. Almost every audition I had done in the past took place in the usual performance area, during off hours. So this was a completely different situation. I remarked to the two managers that I felt like I was on a reality show. They had notepads out while I was playing and singing, and I noticed that they were whispering to each other and making notes. I actually got nervous more than once and had to get myself together. I showcased several different styles, and after about a half hour of playing parts of different songs I said, "Let's talk," and started to pack up. I believed they liked what I presented to them and that I would likely receive a call from them to book some gigs.

Before leaving the hotel I went back to the bar for a cheeseburger. Another indication that they liked me was when the bartender informed me that the manager was taking care of my bill for me. I stayed on their radar by emailing at least once a month for about a year. Even with no response from them at all, I continued to send follow-up emails. My persistence and willingness to audition should pay off for me by landing me a high-paying residual income client.

REFERRALS

Every now and then a new client comes to me through a referral from a previous client.

Last December I received an email from the personal assistant to an executive at Tampa General Hospital asking me to play a holiday party at a mansion in South Tampa, which is a very affluent neighborhood. It was a last-minute request but I happened to be available for the date and the time of the party. The house was incredible and they had catering and bartenders to take care of about eighty guests. This was also good for me because I was able to have a high-end bourbon and some elegant finger food snacks throughout the evening.

When I arrived, I found my contact and was shown where they wanted me to set up. I did not like the spot because it was on wet grass and I would be in pitch dark after sunset. It was very overcast and after two days of rain, the ground was soaked. I talked to the owner about an alternative spot to set up. I was able to move a table about two feet and set up on the back porch, overlooking the pool and yard. I was very happy that they were willing to compromise and the rest of the night went smoothly.

At the end of the evening I was handed an envelope with my pay and was asked if I would like to come to the hospital to play music during the afternoon on Christmas Day. I was delighted to say yes and donate some of my time to make other people happy. There were a lot of smiles and surprised faces in the hospital when I wheeled my cart into the cafeteria area. I played a bunch of happy songs and that day went as well as I had hoped it would. Everyone was very appreciative of me taking time to be there on a holiday. I was on a little bit of a diet at the time, and it was a true test of my will to be able to turn down so many Christmas cookies.

CONTRACTS AND DEPOSITS

I don't use contracts very often, and most places that hire me don't want to use them, either. Most of the booking I do these days is done via email or text message, which is a form of written agreement in itself. These messages can help in situations where there is confusion over the amount of time

I am supposed to play or the amount of money I am to be paid. Very rarely will I need to use them as a contract, but double bookings do happen once in a while and it is nice to pull out my phone and show the manager our confirmation email or text.

Many years ago I was working with a restaurant in Annapolis, Maryland, and I had a string of twelve dates scheduled on one contract. The very first gig of the contract was cancelled due to snow. The manager called me during the afternoon and explained that they were closing because none of their employees could make it due to the storm. I did not want to enforce the contractual obligation and get paid for this particular gig, even though the agreement stipulated that I should. I knew that if I did, they would pull out of the other scheduled dates based on the options in our agreement.

When it came time to play the last gig of this contract, I was able to get paid without playing. Upon arrival the night of the gig, I was told they were going to cancel me because the University of Maryland basketball team was doing well in the NCAA tournament and a lot of people were at the bar to watch the game on TV. I offered to play during halftime and to continue after the game, which they declined. I then proceeded to tell the manager on duty that I had a contract and that I would like to be paid and have my meal while I watched some of the game. After all, I had made the forty-five-minute drive and was on site, ready to go to work. He asked me to provide the contract, so I went to the van and grabbed my backpack with my paperwork inside. When I showed him the contract and explained the situation, he looked kind of unhappy. He told me he needed to contact the general manager and asked me to hang out for a few minutes while he figured out what to do. About fifteen minutes later, he came back with a check for me and said the general manager had told him to honor my contract.

They never wanted to put any more gigs with me on a contract again, and on top of that, it took more than six months to get another booking from them. I did continue to work with them at all three of their locations for several years, but there were no more contracts. Unfortunately, when it comes to bars and restaurants, contracts are pretty much nonexistent. I believe they want to reserve the right to cancel a gig at the last minute for any reason they choose, so that's something to watch out for.

Getting deposits is mostly reserved for private parties and select events. If you can get a deposit, great! I usually ask for at least half pay. This will ensure that if they have to cancel for some reason, I will at least make some money for my time. Whenever this does happen, which is rare, I will take that money and salvage my day by doing something fun, or if I have enough notice I will try to bank the half pay and play another gig. I try to use a deposit to protect myself from losing money if a client changes their mind.

Extra Booking Tip: Do not call or pop in to places to ask for a gig on a Friday or Saturday night, or any time that the business is extremely busy. The owner or manager will probably be annoyed and also wonder why you don't have a gig on the weekend. They will likely remember you for a negative reason, which is not what you want.

Make a checklist of questions to ask. Write down all the information that you want to know before making the call or sending the email. Some questions to keep in mind may include: Will I perform inside or outside? If outside, will I be on a covered stage? What is your pay scale? Do you provide a meal or tab for musicians? If not, do you give a discount to musicians? What days of the week do you hire musicians? What time of day do you schedule live music? How and when do you pay the musicians? Cash, check, or direct deposit? In advance or at the end of the night? Am I allowed to solicit tips with my tip can and set up a merchandise table? Do I load in the front or the back of the location? Does the venue require insurance?

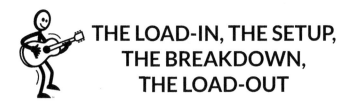

THE LOAD-IN, THE SETUP, THE BREAKDOWN, THE LOAD-OUT

"Musicians should not play music.
Music should play musicians."
—Henry Rollins

In this chapter, I will tell you how I handle these steps on a gig. This is just one way to do them. Every Solo Acoustic Musician will have different gear, a different vehicle, be performing at a different venue, etc. The idea is that each of us can develop a system to make ourselves more efficient and more professional. Over the years I have transitioned from a big van to a four-door sedan to a couple of minivans. I have also used powered and non-powered mixers and speakers. All of these pieces of gear were different shapes and sizes, so I had to make adjustments to my routine. The point is to create strategies and have a plan to make this part of the gig efficient.

THE LOAD-IN AND THE SETUP

One of the first things I do, especially if it is a new venue for me, is to go in and scout out where the electrical outlets are.

Most of the time I will ask for a manager or the contact person for the event and have them show me where they would like me to perform. I may need to grab a twenty-five- or fifty-foot extension cable from the van, depending on how far I will be from an outlet. I organize my gear in my van so that it is easy to quickly load up my cart and get into the venue. I can actually get loaded in and set up in a matter of ten to fifteen minutes most of the time, without rushing.

Sometimes a venue will have an actual stage, and other times I will be told to set up in a corner. Being prepared for any situation is important. If I arrive an hour before my start time and the hostess has just seated eight people at a table in the spot where I am supposed to set up, I have to occupy myself while I wait for them to have their dining experience. When the customers are finally done, the employees will clear and move the table out of my way. That's when I can begin to set up and get on with my show.

Some venues that do provide a stage will have a load-in parking area and a side or backstage door. I really enjoy this! Playing on a stage feels more like an actual show. Even if I have to load in through the front door to get to the stage, I really appreciate the venue's effort and foresight for providing one.

Last week I was playing a brewery where I have worked many times. When I arrived, someone was parked in the loading zone, which is right in front of the door. (They were not unloading by the way... just parked there for the evening and didn't actually leave for a couple hours.) So I had to park up the block and walk to the brewery in a massive downpour and lightning storm. As I mentioned earlier, I keep extra clothes in my van, and I put on a long-sleeved button-up shirt and a baseball cap to stay dry.

I opened my van's back door before getting out. Then I grabbed my guitar case and pedal board case from the back, hit the "close door" button, and ran up the street to the brewery. Then I had to go back to get my cart. I opened the back of the van with my fob as I approached, and was able to stand under the door, mostly safe from the rain, while I expanded my cart and loaded it up inside the van. I used my black tablecloth to cover the contents of my cart, hit the "close door" button again, picked up my cart, set it down on the ground, and moved very quickly toward my destination. I clicked the lock button on my fob as I was moving away from my van. Because I covered my gear, when I got inside the brewery and removed the tablecloth, everything was dry. I was not dry at all, though, and my shoes and socks were soaked the worst. My overshirt and hat were still wet when I started the load-out!

Every place I play has a different area to set up in, and each situation requires me to adapt. I try to establish a somewhat constant routine around the placement of my gear. Since I live and play in Florida, with its summer-like weather nine months of the year, I plug in and place my fans first upon arrival in the stage area. After that, I empty my cart by first placing my tip can and merchandise sign in their spot. Then I place my mic stand, amp, and pedal board where they will be. Then I stow my cases off to the side or in a designated closet. Sometimes I even take my cart, amp case, and pedal board case back to my van. Then I set up one or two of my tables. Usually at some point after I set up my drink table, I get a couple of glasses of water or tea. Then I run my cables, and hook up my mic and iPad. If I am required to provide an extra speaker or plug in to the house system, I will do that last.

I almost always place my AER amp on my right-hand side and my guitar case on my left. I place my mic stand to the left of the pedal board and place my fan, if I am only using one, on my right. As I run my guitar and microphone cables I try to place them neatly and prepare a clean stage area. That is also why I stow away my cart and cases. I try to have some consistency in my routine and the layout of my gear. Of course, every now and then my first fan ends up on the left and so on. It can depend on where the power outlet is. I like to have a routine and know where my gear is so I can act efficiently in the case of emergency, like a broken string or bad weather.

I used to have two speakers and a mixer for my PA system, and would choose a couple of different ways to set up. I liked having one speaker up on a stand and aimed at the audience, while keeping the other on the floor as a monitor aimed at me. In my experience, when a musician puts both of their speakers up on stands and aims them at the audience, a manager will often get complaints about the volume and ask the act to turn down. What I think is happening is that the musician can't hear themselves that well, so they turn the volume up. Then the music is too loud for the audience. By placing one speaker down on the ground, aimed at me, I get a nice loud volume where I am standing, which I like.

I have actually placed both speakers on the floor like monitors before, and the crowd can hear me just fine without it being too loud. It all depends on the shape and size of the room.

I found the AER amp company at a singer-songwriter event. There were several stages and the guy who was running sound where I was playing was providing an AER amp to play through. About five or six years later, I finally purchased one. I bought the 200-watt Compact XL, which was their newest model at the time. I was trying to downsize my gear load to make things easier on myself, and it only weighs about twenty-two pounds. It is an amazing piece of equipment and I have been able to play any size room, outdoor space, and all the venues and events that have hired me with just this one amp.

THE BREAKDOWN AND THE LOAD-OUT

This is pretty much the reverse of the load-in and setup. I can do this part of my gig in less than ten minutes and be ready to leave. The only factor that varies is the distance from the stage to my van.

The first thing I do is put my guitar away in its case and pack up all the accessories that live in the guitar case with it. This includes my iPad and iPad holder, microphone, towels, drink holder, any tools, and any other items from the accessories list that fit in my case. I get my cart and cases from wherever I've stowed them. I unplug everything except my fans. I put away my AER amp first and then wrap up all my cables, placing them on my pedal board. Basically, I continue loading up my cart in the reverse of the way it was loaded on the way in. I do it the same every time.

When I get back to my van, everything goes in its place very quickly. I have seen musicians throw all their gear into the van in random order before. I prefer to have my things organized and in their place. I always know where everything is and that is important for avoiding mistakes like leaving your mic stand behind, or forgetting to grab your extension cord.

This leads me to the last two steps of the load-out. First do a "Dummy Check." This is just a walk through the stage area to make sure you are not leaving any of your things behind. I can't believe how many musicians leave things behind, but it happens. Every now and then during load-ins and setups I find mic stands and cables in the stage area. I usually turn them in to the manager on duty and asked who played last, probably the day before. I might know the musician and can reach out to them and tell them I found their gear.

Once, I left the side table I use for merch and/or my drinks behind at one of my regular gigs. The next day I called the restaurant and was told by the manager that it was in the office. He mentioned that they knew for sure it was mine because of all the stickers I have on it. So here's another tip for you. Label your gear with a sticker or use a paint marker to put your name on it somewhere. It might help you get it back if you leave something behind.

Second, and believe it or not this is very important, clean up after yourself. Make sure to leave no trash on the stage area or wherever you set up. I don't like it when I show up to play a gig and I have to clear away empty glasses, bottles, and broken strings left by the previous act. I have played a place about once a month on a Saturday night from six to ten PM for some time. They also hire a band for the afternoon shift on Saturdays from one to five. These guys are a four- or five-piece and when they pack up they just leave all their trash behind. I have not "thrown them under the bus" with the management there, but I have been booking myself on Friday nights for a while. They do not have an early act on Fridays, and the stage is always clean when I get there.

I have been told by waitresses and bar staff over the years that they appreciate the fact that I clean up after myself. They have also conveyed to me that other musicians don't do the same. Believe me, they notice who leaves behind trash. Who do you think has to clean up after you? It is kind of like the rule about arriving on time; people will take notice of what you are doing and your work ethic. It's just another small step in being a professional Solo Acoustic Musician.

I always pack up and load out before I get paid, settle my bill, or hang out with friends. I have seen musicians go to the bar and hang out for a while before packing up. I do not go about my business this way. If I choose to hang out for an hour after my gig, and have a beer with friends or fans, I will already be loaded out and done with my work for the evening. It is especially important to load out quickly if another musician is playing on the same stage after me.

BEFORE THE GIG, ON THE GIG, AFTER THE GIG

The true beauty of music is that it connects
people. It carries a message,
and we, the musicians are the messengers.
—Roy Ayers

BEFORE THE GIG

This can obviously be different for every person but I have a few things I like to do before a gig...

I don't like to eat right before I perform. I don't like getting up on stage on a full belly. So I usually have a meal well before arriving at the venue. Sometimes I like to have about half a cup of coffee before starting to play. Another thing I like to do pre-show sometimes is to sit in my van with the A/C on and close my eyes. This is especially helpful after setting up in extreme heat. I can relax and cool down before going up on stage to perform. I will also do this on my breaks sometimes. It just helps to have my own quiet place to refocus my energy.

Believe it or not, a few short sprints, some pushups, or jumping jacks before a set can be a great warm-up for a gig.

It really doesn't take much to get the blood flowing and bring your energy levels up. I don't typically do a bunch of vocal exercises before the gig because I will start with easy songs and build up as I go. I do this because the gig is going to be three to four hours of singing and I want to pace myself. When I do a one-hour gig for something like an all-original show, then I will do vocal warm-ups.

I was on a gig in Fell's Point, Maryland, which is a night-life bar district in Baltimore when I met Gavin Rossdale on the sidewalk. I was pretty early so I went ahead and set up. Then I stepped out for a minute to see who was playing at some of the other bars that night. A Lexus sedan pulled up to the corner and a man in jeans, a denim jacket, and a black T-shirt, with long grey hair, hopped out of one side of the car. He walked around to open the door for the passenger in the back seat. Out of the car emerged Gavin Rossdale! I said hi and he introduced himself. We actually stood there and talked for a few minutes.

This was around 2006 or 2007, and he was on a break from making music with Bush. He was touring with a new band—I can't remember their name. They were playing Ram's Head Live, a well-known music venue in downtown Baltimore. I remember that he mentioned that he thought that was a funny name for a venue. I was hoping he would offer me tickets to the show, but it didn't happen. The conversation ended and we went our separate ways. It was still a cool experience to meet a famous rock star on the sidewalk outside of my gig.

ON THE GIG

Upon arriving at a gig, especially if it is my first time playing there, I look over the situation before I load in. I might go in and take a quick walk around and see if I can guess where I might be setting up. Then I will ask a manager to show me where they would like me to set up and play. I next ask where the electrical outlet is, followed by if they have a house speaker system they would like me to plug into. I wasn't used to this second question until I moved to Florida. Many of the locations I play here have a house system I can plug into, so that my music is heard throughout the entire establishment.

Some of them don't work so well after about a year of crazy Florida weather, but most places are in a habit of replacing their speakers yearly. It's just part of the cost of doing business and having live music. They probably write it off on their taxes to offset the cost of the new ones.

How we act on a gig is important.

Watching your volume level is a hotly discussed topic among musicians and management. Some people will always complain about anything. So unfortunately, we draw a lot of attention by "making noise"... When I am discussing the issue with a manager on duty, I will ask if it was a patron that complained or if it is their personal preference. I will also make sure to point out my volume knob and show them I am turning it down a little right in front of them. After years of having this conversation, I have heard all the stories. Managers complaining that a musician turned down and then turned back up, etc. The squeaky wheel, the complaining customer, gets the attention.

You can always help yourself when discussing these situations by staying calm and offering solutions. Keep an eye on the room. If you see bartenders leaning way over the bar to take orders from customers, then the room is too loud. Notice that I didn't say the musician's volume was too loud.

Another unfortunate side effect of being a musician in the corner of the restaurant is that we are blamed for the whole room's volume level. There are times when the "white noise" of the crowd is so loud that I can't hear myself at all. These days, I just smile and play as best I can. I know I will have good and bad gigs along the way and some things are just out of my control. I have to maintain and go with the flow. I can always re-evaluate a client or venue, and if I don't like playing there I can move on and find another place to play.

There have been several times where I have been on a gig and have been told a few times to turn down. Each time I am asked, I turn down the volume on my PA system. Then when I go on break or when I am finished and start packing up, an employee of the bar turns on the house music and it is much louder than I was. I remember one incident where a bartender actually got into a yelling match with the manager over the way I was treated. He was mad at the manager for telling me to turn down and then cranking up the music extremely loud when I went on a break. In my opinion, it doesn't make any sense, but it happens from time to time.

I have even experienced a similar situation with the owner of an establishment I was playing. Upon arrival and at the start of the load-in, I made a note to myself that the "white noise" of the people in the bar was very loud. After the second song of my first set, the owner asked me to please turn down my volume. I did so, only to be approached two more times and asked to turn down more. Each time, I turned my volume down... By that point, I was so quiet I couldn't really hear myself because of the loud crowd noise, and guess who the loudest person in the room was? That's right, the owner. Her table consisted of her and about eight friends who were drinking shots and acting out, basically yelling their conversations and laughing as loudly as they could.

Sometimes people really appreciate what we do as musical entertainers, and other times a gig can be just about getting through it and getting that paycheck. It is part of life to have good days and bad days.

HUMIDITY AND STAYING IN TUNE

There will be days when it is so humid that I will struggle to keep my guitar in tune even indoors. I can hear it happening halfway through the song. I will stop to tune after every song, only to hear my B string going flat as I start playing again. There is not much I can do about it other than to stop, tune again, and get on with it.

BROKEN STRING PROTOCOL

I am prepared for the rare times when I break a string. I keep a binder with single guitar strings in it in my guitar case, along with a couple of string winders and a pair of clippers that I use to cut off the excess string. Whenever I break a string, I just stay calm, get out my binder and my tools, and solve the problem. I don't rush, and I am back playing in a couple of minutes.

I met legendary basketball coach Pat Riley on a Fourth of July gig in Aspen, Colorado, in the late '90s. The city was shooting fireworks off the mountainside and all of downtown was packed with people. I took a break from my gig to go outside and watch the fireworks with everyone else. I was lucky enough to be able to find a bench to sit on and relax, so

I headed straight toward it. I looked down to my left as I was walking toward the bench I wanted to sit on. That's when I noticed a person I thought looked like Pat Riley.

I sat down on the empty bench directly across from him. Two random people approached me and asked if they could share the bench, too. Of course I said yes, and we all sat and enjoyed the fireworks. A few minutes went by and I asked them if they thought it was him, but they didn't know who Pat Riley was. I explained that he coached the Los Angeles Lakers in the '80s, the New York Knicks in the early '90s, and at that time he was coaching the Miami Heat.

The man I suspected of being Pat Riley was sitting on a bench with a little boy and talking to a woman who was sitting with a little girl on the bench next to him. I had put it together that they were his wife and children. After a little bit they got up and started to walk away down the pedestrian walking area in downtown. He then stopped, leaned over and said something to the woman, and turned around. He started walking straight towards me, so I stood up. He extended his hand and said, "Happy Fourth of July."

I shook his hand and said, "It's very nice to meet you, Coach. Same to you." Then he walked away.

I guess he figured out that I knew who he was, but that I was polite enough not to bother him while he was celebrating a national holiday with his wife and kids. I thought it was very cool of him to take just a minute and say hello. After the fireworks, I went back into the bar and played more songs.

The Fourth of July has always been one of my favorite holidays!

AFTER THE GIG

I like to eat dinner after the gig. Most nights I get dinner to go, stop off for food on the road, or cook when I get home. It's a big part of my routine. Every night when I back my van into the driveway I have a couple of things that I like to do. I make sure I carry my guitar, amp, and pedal board inside the house. If I am using my mixer and a speaker, I bring them in as well. Electronics do not do well in the constant heat where I live. I usually leave my mic stand, speaker stand, small tables, and merchandise box in the van overnight, but everything else must come inside.

A friend of mine left two PA speakers in his car for two weeks in August here in Florida and then wondered why they didn't work anymore. But besides the danger of heat from the sun, we also need to think about theft. I have known musicians who leave their gear in a car or van overnight all the time, but I have always been an advocate of bringing my gear in the house.

While loading out at a rooftop bar in Clearwater Beach, Florida, I met Hulk Hogan. I had seen him around town a few times, either riding his scooter down Mandalay Avenue or walking into shops off the main drag. At another beach resort, when I was playing by the pool and tiki bar, he and his friends were being seated on the outside second floor balcony of the fancy restaurant on site. I was too far away to say hi and I wasn't going to interrupt his dinner for an autograph.

This time was different. I had just stepped into the elevator with my cart and guitar on my way downstairs to the parking garage. Then I heard a woman's voice say, "Hold the elevator, please." I put my hand out to stop the door from closing and Hulk Hogan and friends walked into the elevator with me. I had to tell him that I watched him when I was a kid and that it would be an honor to shake his hand.

At the same rooftop bar, I met former Tampa Bay Buccaneers head coach John Gruden. When I went on a break, I made my way over to his table and said, "Nice to meet you, Coach." Nothing fancy, just a simple hello. I really don't want to bother a celebrity, especially when I am on the job.

Unfortunately, that place does not have live music anymore. It still has an amazing view from the tenth-floor rooftop bar, though.

 # WORKING THE CROWD

"It's nice when you know the crowd are on your side. I can only repay them by working my hardest when I do get on and trying to impress them."
—Alex Oxlade-Chamberlain

Working the crowd usually starts with picking the right songs. I have hundreds of songs in my book and I pick the next one as I go. Throughout the gig I am trying to determine what I think the people in front of me would like to hear. While I am on stage, I look out across the crowd and analyze a few factors: what age group or demographic is in front of me, what style of clothing the people are wearing, and if I think they are locals or visitors. I can usually guess that people in my parents' age group will like the Beatles. I try that out and if it works, I will play a few more songs from that era. When I see someone in the audience wearing beach clothes, which happens a lot, I will play a Jimmy Buffett or Bob Marley song. It is also fun to see someone wearing a band T-shirt and then play a song by that band.

Another way to engage the crowd is to talk to them. Look for openings, like someone wearing a sports team's hat or shirt. I will ask people with a Phillies shirt on if they are from

Philadelphia. If they say yes, I ask them if they like Pat's or Geno's? This is always fun because these two cheesesteak places are huge rivals and everyone from Philly knows about it. By engaging people in the audience, you become approachable to them, which means they will feel more comfortable talking to you and making requests. It makes it easier to find out what they like, and hopefully earns you tips.

I recently started a conversation between songs with the people at a table directly in front of me and asked them where they were from. "Are you local, or are you visiting?" They told me they were from San Antonio, Texas, and I proceeded to play "Folsom Prison Blues" by the late, great Johnny Cash, because he references going down to San Antone. In the same song, he makes a reference to Reno. The next time I meet some people from Nevada, I will remember to slip that song into my set for them.

Just the other day, a guy wearing a Tom Petty T-shirt walked into the bar I was playing . So I knew right away what that dude liked and started playing "Into the Great Wide Open." As I started singing the song, he turned around with a big smile on his face and yelled out, "Rock 'n' roll, brother!" I can appreciate his enthusiasm because Tom Petty and the Heartbreakers were an all-time great band who wrote many great songs. At that same gig, another man arrived wearing a Harley Davidson T-shirt from a Bike Week in Daytona some years back. I slipped Neil Young's song "Unknown Legend" into my set. It's a slow ballad and nobody was really paying attention until I made it to the chorus. This is when the song references Harley-Davidson. It always grabs the attention of people in the crowd who are wearing Harley shirts or jackets, and it works really well when there is a group of them together in the audience.

> "Music is probably the only real magic I have encountered in my life. There's not some trick involved in it. It's pure and it's real. It moves, it heals, it communicates, and does all these incredible things."
> —Tom Petty

Making eye contact is another good way to engage the crowd. I will look from left to right and find people who are paying attention and make eye contact. I will follow this up by smiling at them. Very often this simple gesture changes the course of the gig. Never underestimate the power of looking at someone and making an exchange. It's another way to make yourself approachable, and that leads to happier audience members.

Sometimes while I am playing lead over a loop, I will use my eyes to communicate with the audience. Then I will use my mouth to mimic the notes I am playing, making silly, fun faces when I am playing. It creates a certain amount of entertainment value and makes people laugh. It really makes kids giggle. I love the smiles on children's faces as they laugh and dance in front of me while I am playing happy songs for them. I will set a loop with a beat to it and dance along with them while I am on stage. I get a lot of positive energy from this kind of audience interaction.

While talking to the audience and making eye contact with them works wonders, I will take it up a notch sometimes when I go on break by randomly fist-bumping or high-fiving people in the audience. It's especially fun to do this with kids. Even when I am on stage I will try to get some high fives and fist bumps from people passing by on their way in or out of the venue.

Getting kids to dance is another good way to work the crowd and get their parents to tip you. If you have happy songs in your song list, use them. I will deliberately ask the kids in front of me, "Would you like to hear a happy song?" They almost always say yes, and I will play "Three Little Birds" by Bob Marley. I will tell you that pretty much every time I do this, the children will sing along and start dancing with me. The parents will sing along too, and now I have broken through a barrier between me and the crowd. It becomes easier to follow this up with more talking and eye contact. It's a great icebreaker that actually pays off with money and applause.

I have another trick that I will share and that is to try a funny song or a joke. I don't always land it right, and sometimes I bomb. The thing is, though, I am not scared of failing at trying to be funny. Not every crowd is going to be into it. When it works, though, it is an awesome feeling. The timing has to be right and that is all up to the performer's sense of the situation. I have found that the best time to use this tactic is later in the gig, when people have had a few drinks and hopefully are already into the music you have been playing for them.

What we as Solo Acoustic Musicians would like to happen: We play songs and the audience likes them... they clap and applaud while filling our tip cans full of dollar bills. Sometimes, you may play a few songs in a row that you think were awesome. You are really giving your all, but you get no response. Right in front of you are people, physical people, and they simply do not respond at all... but they are listening. It's hard to do, but we can't take it personally. Most places we play are not music venues or listening rooms. People are there to eat, drink, and engage in conversation. I know it's hard to have a beer or a cheeseburger in your hand and then start clapping for a musician.

When I am out on a night off and happen to be in a place where a musician is playing, I will start clapping at the end of their songs. It almost always gets other people to join in and clap with me. After four or five songs in a row, the other people tend to start clapping more regularly. So, next time you are out and listening to a live musician, do them a favor and clap at the end of the songs.

ATTITUDE

"Quality performance starts with a positive attitude."
—*Jeffrey Gitomer*

Attitude is a choice, so always try to stay humble, kind, and be positive. When you show up to a gig, have confidence that you will be well received. Your resolve will be tested, but you should try to maintain a positive outlook no matter how the gig is going. I have employed several techniques to try to keep me in a good mood, but the most important one is the first thing I do and it is simple. I smile. That's it. Smiling is contagious and when I smile at the audience, positive reactions usually follow. It just seems to lighten the mood in the room.

Sometimes it is tough, when you are playing your heart out and think you are really doing well, only to garner no response from the crowd. A few songs in a row with nobody clapping or even acknowledging you at all can start to make you question what you are doing. You have to always remember that the people you are playing for are probably trying to enjoy a night out with friends and family. They are probably talking and eating dinner while having some drinks to unwind. We as musicians cannot take it personally when the audience doesn't clap after every song. I try to notice the amount of people nodding their heads and tapping their feet while they are eating and having conversations. This can help me when I don't feel I am being heard or listened to. When I notice these things, I can usually just smile and play a really happy song. This will usually remedy the situation by engaging the crowd.

REQUESTS

I get requests all the time, and they can come at any time during a gig. Some will be made politely between songs and some will be yelled out during a song. There are times when people are downright rude and will walk up to me while I am singing a song to request that I play a different song. It is a challenge to stay calm while performing the song I am playing. Even after years onstage, I still find it really rude. In my mind, there is a basic protocol for making a request of a performing musician and some people don't know it, get it, or seem to care. They are even more rude if they are intoxicated. But I don't take it personally at all and conduct myself as professionally as I can.

I can initiate the request when I am engaging the crowd. This can happen from the stage or when I am on a break and talking with people. I find a helpful technique is to try to direct the request as best I can based on my song list and knowing my wheelhouse. A lot of times when I ask people in the crowd if they have any requests, this will put them on the spot and they will draw a blank. This allows me to say that I am going to play another song and if they want to think about what they might like to hear, they can ask me in between songs. This helps to control the impulsiveness of some patrons and also makes me accessible to the audience. At that point they become more at ease about interacting with me.

When audience members ask, "Do you take requests?" I like to say, "Yes, I do. Although fulfilling them is a whole other issue that I discuss with my therapist on Thursday afternoon." I pause for a smile or giggle, and then I follow up by saying, "I have been telling that joke for years now, and I don't actually have a therapist, but I guess if I did it would be on Thursday afternoons." I find it to be a good icebreaker and a way to take control of the conversation and the forthcoming request. I will take a minute and tell them that we can talk about it and find a common ground for me to play some songs that I know just for them.

The vaguer the request the better. Like someone asking for a happy song, or a bluesy song, or a country song. These are the best because I can scroll through my book and find something quickly. When someone asks for a specific song or artist it gets tougher. If you don't know the song, you can try a different song or artist in the same genre or time period as a compromise.

The psychology of a request took a long time for me to understand. As far as I am concerned, when someone makes a specific song request, they are trying to trigger a memory. Smell is the number one memory trigger according to the textbooks, but I believe that songs are right up there. Something happens when we hear certain songs that can trigger subconscious memories or feelings. Maybe a certain smell will remind you of your grandmother's cooking or

Christmas with your family. I think songs can and do have the same effect on us and can inspire us to feel a particular emotion or vibe.

When someone requests a song you don't know, but you do know a song by another artist that is from a similar genre or era, that compromise may still provide that nostalgic feeling for the person.

"Music, at its essence, is what gives us memories. And the longer a song has existed in our lives, the more memories we have of it."
—Stevie Wonder

I was once berated for over thirty minutes by a loud drunk who could not believe that I didn't know any Bon Jovi songs. He proceeded to play air guitar and sing parts of the song he wanted to hear, extremely loudly. Five feet in front of me while I was playing a different song was a drunk man yelling, "Wanted Dead or Alive." It was a major distraction but I continued playing. Eventually I got to the point in my set where I could take a break and he left the venue. I am assuming he went somewhere else to find someone else to heckle. It still makes me laugh when I talk with other musicians and friends about things like that.

Nowadays, people will ask me for a song I don't know and then say, "You can just look it up on your phone and play it, do it now." This happened to me recently. The song in question was brand-new and by an artist I was not familiar with. So even if I did look up the chord chart with lyrics I wouldn't have any idea about the melody or rhythm. It's pretty hard to produce a song in that scenario. I explained nicely to the man that I had never even heard the song. So while I was playing my next song, he stepped in front of me with his phone pointed at me and the song playing, as if this was a normal way to go about making a request. I laugh at stuff like this and have fun talking with other musicians and friends about these situations. Even though I am very experienced, it still blows my mind when it happens. I am comforted by hearing other musicians with similar tales, and knowing that I am not the only one it happens to.

The drunk woman saying "play something I can dance to" can almost never give me an example of a song that she can dance to. When it happens that the woman *does* have an example of a song she can dance to, it is a song that a SAM wouldn't be able to do without a drummer, or is inappropriate for the venue and would not be received positively by the owner or manager if I did play it.

One of the most annoying requests is when someone asks you to play a song that you don't like. But what's even worse is when someone requests a song that I don't want to play, and then they leave while I am playing it. It makes me laugh at this point in my career, but it used to bug me. I don't understand how someone can ask you to play a song and then leave the room when you are playing it! They might just go to the bathroom, but sometimes they leave the venue altogether—I have seen both scenarios. Be prepared for all kinds of rude behavior like this. If you are prepared for people to do things like that, it will bother you a lot less at the end of the day.

Every now and then someone surprises me with their request and their reaction to my version of the song. A man in his seventies walked up to me at one gig. He didn't wait until I was done and I literally had to stop playing the song I was playing to talk with him. It was very rude of him, but I just smiled and listened. I used my tuner pedal to mute the song I had playing on a loop.

He began by asking me if I knew any songs from the '60s. I told him I didn't really think I had many. Then he proceeded to list band names. Eventually he said the Rolling Stones. I told him that I knew one Rolling Stones song and that I would play it right after I finished the song I was currently in the middle of. He walked back to his table and I stepped on my pedal and played the rest of the song.

The song I played for him was "Wild Horses." I noticed that a few times during the song, the man would point at me and say something negative to the other people at his table. I could tell it was negative by his facial expressions and body language. So I was not surprised at all that after a few more songs, he approached me again. After accusing me of ripping him off and threatening to take back the three dollars he had placed in my tip can, he yelled that I was a no-good talentless hack who didn't play a Rolling Stones song for him.

I calmly stated, into the microphone, that I had played "Wild Horses" by the Rolling Stones for him. His reply was a very loud and emphatic, "That is not a Rolling Stones song!" To which I replied, "You can't always get what you want." The other audience members burst out laughing and the man huffed and puffed his way to the manager to complain. The manager and I had a good laugh about it later. It is hard to get it right all the time, but every now and then I have a quick wit and end up on the right side of things.

UPBEAT VS. UP-TEMPO

For years I would have conversations with other musicians about requests to play something upbeat. This would almost always be followed by the musician playing something very fast. A better option is to play something happy, or something the requesting audience knows and really likes. It doesn't have to be fast. Although I have had some people say they want both happy and fast.

Hecklers are usually drunk and annoying. Try to stay humble and kind, and never curse into the microphone if you can help it. Most of the time, just ignoring hecklers is sufficient. But every now and then, someone crosses the line. The venue staff and the crowd will usually have your back and help you deal with the situation, but there are so many random variables that it is really a case-by-case thing and you will have to do what you think is appropriate at the time. Always stand up for yourself, and show respect for yourself and the establishment that hired you.

TAKE A LONGER BREAK

Being asked to take a longer break is an unusual request, to say the least. Most of the time I am asked to shorten my break times, or I will hear complaints from owners and managers about other musicians who have been taking excessively long breaks. But in some rare instances, I have been asked to go on a longer break. The first time this happened, I was ten minutes into my second set when the manager came over to the stage and asked me to go take a forty-minute break. I didn't understand and I asked why he wanted me to do that.

I was told that people were lingering to hear more music, but that they weren't spending any more money. As a matter of fact, most of the patrons had actually paid their entire bill and were just staying to listen. The manager went on to explain that there was an hour-long wait to get a table and they needed to turn the tables over. I unplugged my guitar, put it in my case, and turned on the house stereo system. Then I went to my van, kicked up the AC, and chilled out. I came back into the restaurant thirty minutes later and sure enough I had a whole new batch of customers on the deck to play for. This is usually going to help me make more tips overall for the night because I have new patrons to work with.

In a way, this is a huge compliment and a clear indication that I am doing something right. If people are sticking around and staying longer to hear me play more songs, it means that they like what I am doing. This has actually happened about ten more times in the last two years and at three different venues. I enjoy the fact that I play some popular places that have a large regular customer base as well as a constant stream of tourists. When people are staying longer and not spending more money, then not only is the venue not bringing in more money, but the servers are not getting new customers and therefore losing out on tips. It's a win-win for me, as I get a longer break.

GOING THROUGH THE MOTIONS

With the number of gigs that I play every year, it can be easy for my energy level to wane. Sometimes, too, the attention to detail that I am supposed to apply to my craft can slip. It is totally up to me to realize this and adjust. I don't have a coach in a corner of the ring, like a boxer, to yell at me to pick up my energy. I try to be aware of situations that are distracting or that can be energy draining. I also have a system in place to get me back on track. I have a handful of songs that really make me happy, and when things are getting stale for me on stage I will play one of these "go-to" songs. Playing one will usually get me back in a good mood, more focused, and in the right mental frame to put on a better set. I really want you to try to pay attention to your energy trends throughout your performance. I strive to have fun and entertain, and I don't want to just "go through the motions" just to make my paycheck.

 # WEATHER

"It is only in sorrow bad weather masters us;
in joy we face the storm and defy it."
—Amelia Barr

"Is it going to rain?"

I have asked this question and had this conversation hundreds of times. At this point in my career, if I know that it's going to rain then I follow the protocol laid out by the place. Each establishment will have different rules about weather. Some will cancel you outright. Some will have an alternate spot for you to set up and play inside. (This is what we hope for!) It never bothers or upsets me to be cancelled because of bad weather. I will just salvage the rest of the day by doing something I enjoy. As I write this, it's Sunday and I am supposed to be performing at a place on the beach from seven to ten PM, but I've just received a text that my gig is cancelled because of rain and lightning. I guess I will be typing a little more today than I had scheduled.

RAIN ON THE GIG

Nothing is worse than the stress of putting your gear at risk. If you can acquire really good, expensive gear then you have to protect it. One way I have learned to cope with the possibility of impending storms is to have a rain-optional PA system. My secondary PA setup consists of two Mackie 1000-watt powered speakers and a small Alesis mixer. I would rather put older or less valuable gear at risk of getting rained on. Remember, always buy two of everything and have backup gear.

The first thing to do if it does start raining while you are playing is stop, turn everything off, and unplug all the power cables. All of your gear has a chance of drying out and being OK if it gets a little wet. But when gear is plugged in and powered up, it can be permanently destroyed if it gets soaked. Believe me when I say I have a little experience dealing with unpredictable Florida weather. We have a rainy season here in the summer where it rains every day and sometimes several times a day.

If I am pretty sure it's going to rain at some point, I will write the set list on a small piece of paper so I won't put my iPad at risk. The short list will consist of songs I can do great versions of without a need for lyrics or chord charts. I won't set up my iPod, which I use to play music on my breaks, either. Basically, when there's a high probability of rain, I eliminate things I normally set up in case I have to break down very quickly. The less I set up, the less I have to worry about, protect, and move quickly to a dry place.

When arriving at a new venue, bar, or restaurant, after finding out where they want me to set up, I will offer suggestions for alternate placement if I think there is a high probability of rain. Being near a door that leads inside is great. Some kind of roof overhead is always appreciated. I want to know that if a storm pops up quickly I have a safe place to go in a hurry, and I want to know how far and how fast I need to move my equipment and myself to safety. I have several different ways of preparing for a mid-gig emergency that can happen suddenly, and it is best to be prepared with some kind of contingency plan.

The cart I use is raised off the ground on wheels, and all of my gear except my guitar case will fit into it. I keep a tarp and bungee cables in the van so that I can quickly put my gear into the cart and cover it with my tarp. Sometimes when I am loading in I will put the tarp and bungee cables into the cart so they are already on the stage with me rather than left in the van. If I am on an outside stage with a roof I will move my cart to the middle of the stage area to get as much roof coverage as I can. I am sure you know how that sideways rain likes to change direction with the wind.

Never forget that you are an independent contractor and the owner of your own business. This means that ultimately it is your choice when it comes to setting up or breaking down because of weather. If you arrive on site and don't think you should set up at all, you get to make that decision. Most owners and managers I work with understand my choices and respect my decisions. But there are some out there that do not care about my point of view. Remember, it is your gear that you need to protect. I would rather lose one night of pay by not setting up in bad weather than damaging my gear so badly I can't work again until it's repaired or even replaced.

There are some musicians who will put trash bags over their gear. I am not one of them. I play one venue that likes musicians to bring an extra speaker to put outside. I am setting up and playing inside, but part of their deck seating area is right outside the door and window I am standing next to. The restaurant is right in the middle of a bustling downtown area. So the external speaker helps bring people in. Believe it or not, it actually does the job.

One day it started raining and I quickly brought my speaker inside. One of the bartenders asked me if I wanted a trash bag to put over it, to which I replied no. Then the owner came over and asked the same question. I explained that the purpose of having an extension speaker outside was to draw in people who are walking by on the sidewalk, and that during this downpour there were no people walking by. She agreed and said I made a good point. On a normal sunny day in this town, though, there would have been a ton of foot traffic and the extra speaker would have created interest in her location.

Many years ago in Washington, DC, I was playing in a bar in the Adams Morgan district. This is an area filled with lots of bars, restaurants, and shops, and it has a lot of foot traffic over a several-block radius. It is a popular destination for people going out for the night. Now, I was playing inside this time, but it had been raining all day. I even got soaked walking back to the bar after parking my van several blocks away.

I was on a small stage in front of the bar, standing in a large bay-window-type area, opening for a local band whose gear was already set up behind me. Halfway through my set, the roof caved in a little, right above the drum set behind me. The next thing we knew, water was pouring in, all over the drums. That was the end of my set! I proceeded to help move things off the stage and dry off some of their gear. That was a crazy thing to happen while playing an indoor show!

Something similar happened to me more recently. I arrived at a brewery that I like to play, about half an hour north of where I live. When I got inside I was shocked to find a leak from the roof dripping onto the stage. There was a huge storm with a massive amount of lightning strikes that evening, and it was raining hard everywhere. It's no wonder that there were several leaks in the roof of the building. I found the owner and asked for a bucket and a towel for the stage. After he mopped up the puddle, I laid down the towel and placed the bucket on the stage where the rain was dripping. This contained the problem and allowed me to set up. The wet spot was in front of stage right and wasn't going to be in my way while I performed, but I wanted to make sure that precautions were taken in advance in case the situation got worse. It was more than an hour before the rain and the leak let up, but the storm did eventually settle down and the drip stopped.

OPPOSITE OF RAIN... IN THE HOT SUN

"Like sunshine, music is a powerful force
that can instantly and almost chemically
change your entire mood."
—Michael Franti

Living in the Tampa Bay area of Florida, it is hot! We have summer-like conditions for about nine months of the year. I know for a fact that the summer in Connecticut is just as hot for a couple of months. Musicians there deal with the same things we do here during that time. Indeed, musicians any-where will have to deal with weather on some gigs. Standing in the hot sun for several hours with a guitar can be intolerable and exhausting. I try to only work with places that will adjust or already provide a roof or cover of some kind. I like to play whether it's rain or shine, but it doesn't always work out that way.

Our gear doesn't like the rain or the heat, but owners and managers do not always seem to take into account that we are risking our expensive equipment. I will take the time to explain to them if I have to, because many don't realize the sun can damage our gear. I know a few musicians who have had speakers and even mixers quit working on them in the middle of a show because of direct sunlight. In the past I have been known to cover my speakers and/or mixer with towels or T-shirts to help absorb the sun and heat. I keep extra towels and T-shirts in the van for other reasons, but this can be another use for them. If you find yourself in direct sunlight on a gig, I implore you to apply this strategy to avoid having a piece of equipment overheat or short out. If you don't have towels with you, ask the venue manager for some.

When I was younger, I built a cardboard box for my pedal board that would keep the sun from hitting it. I was playing at a beach bar and the stage was in direct sunlight. It was a steady four-to-eight PM gig, and that was a lot of sun exposure for me and my gear. The first time I played there, I couldn't read the lights on my pedals and when I was packing up, I was shocked at how hot my pedals were. That night I came up with the idea of a box with a half lid to shade my pedals from the sun. The next day I could see the lights and they did not get nearly as hot as they had the day before.

Upon arrival for a private event in a client's backyard, I was shown to the spot they wanted me to set up and play. It was in direct sunlight, and I wasn't happy at all. I looked around and started making alternative suggestions until we settled on a spot that was shaded by a couple of trees. I would be about ten feet farther away from the guests, but I would be more comfortable and could just turn my volume up a little if I needed to be louder.

Weather is always going to be a concern on a gig. It can even affect a gig that is being played inside. When I lived up north, shows would sometimes be cancelled because of snow. I would be ready and able to load out to my van, drive there, and do my show, only to be told the venue would be closing for the night because their employees and customers could not make it there. This can happen sometimes, and I guess I can't blame them for having to close because of the circumstances.

In Florida, I have been cancelled because of rain even though the stage area was under a roof. The reasoning behind the decision was explained to me by a manager. He said that there was so much rain, and the majority of their seating was uncovered, so they would be unable to accommodate customers and it would be too slow to afford to pay me based on the inevitable bad turnout. I want to play my gigs and get paid, but it doesn't make financial sense for a venue to pay me when they are not bringing in any money. They see it as a loss. Also, I really don't want to perform to an empty room—it's not very much fun.

I try to work through the problems that weather can provide while protecting my equipment and providing a quality product and service. As a Solo Acoustic Musician, I encounter many types of situations due to the weather. Some of them will be predicted by the weatherman and some will pop up on me at the last minute. I try to be prepared and have systems in place to deal with anything I may encounter.

 **WHEN THINGS GO WRONG**

You can never run out of things that can go wrong.
—Murphy's Law

Although I am writing a book in hopes of helping other Solo Acoustic Musicians be able to do what I do and become a pro at it, I do make mistakes. I am very good at being a SAM, but I am not perfect.

INSURANCE

Do you need insurance? What do you need it for? What kind of insurance do you need? As a SAM, you may be required to have insurance to work with certain clients. It is always good to have insurance. We all recognize that we need car insurance, health insurance, dental insurance, life insurance, renter's insurance, home insurance, etc. It is a long list for sure, so it only makes sense that it would be smart to cover ourselves with some kind of insurance when we are performing.

Although 99% of my clients do not ask for or require me to provide proof of insurance, I have it and am prepared with paperwork if I am asked. The first time I purchased insurance for performers and entertainers, I had to ask why it was required of me. The manager at the resort explained that while he trusted me to be professional on the job site, it was possible that something abnormal could happen. One example he gave me was that the wind could knock my speaker stand over with a speaker on it and it could land on a person. Or maybe a person could trip over a piece of my equipment or a cable or extension cord and be injured. I thought these explanations were kind of silly but I could also understand his concern.

As a SAM, I don't think I have much of a chance of harming someone while performing. I am not juggling knives or using fire in my act. I do not bring audience members on stage with me or engage in any dangerous activities. But just in case, I have insurance coverage.

You will need to buy commercial liability insurance, and $1,000,000 of coverage is standard. I have purchased liability insurance from two companies in the past. I have researched several other companies as well, and all of them have a similar price point. You should be able to get covered for $300 or less for a year at a time.

Specialty Insurance Agency - specialtyinsuranceagency.com

Verifly - verifly.com

This company has an app you can install on your phone. They offer insurance by the hour, day, month, and multiple months. Their app could come in handy if I find myself needing insurance when I arrive at a new gig. In just a few minutes, I will be insured for the gig.

FORGOTTEN GUITAR

One morning last spring I was driving to a gig at Tampa International Airport. I was on time and found a parking spot in the garage near the elevators. As I was unloading my van and filling up my cart it suddenly dawned on me that I did not have my guitar with me!

The first thing I did was put my gear back into my van and pull out my phone to call the agency that booked me. There was no answer. I guessed that it was too early for anyone to be in the office, so I tried the owner's cell number and once again I got no response. My next play was to call one of the two cell numbers that I had for the airport representatives with whom I had worked previously. As I was pulling out of the parking garage, I finally got someone on the phone. I explained what was going on and that I would return as soon as I could and start right away. She told me to drive safely and everything would be fine when I got back.

I drove a little more aggressively than usual, but still safely, and went all the way home to get my guitar. I was pretty embarrassed upon my return but I set up and played music for all the people coming through the main terminal that day. I believe I started out with Bobby McFerrin's song "Don't Worry, Be Happy." This song always calms me down, puts a smile on my face, and gets me into a good mood. I definitely needed to de-stress and cool down.

I was scheduled to play from ten AM to noon, take a two-hour break, and play again from two to four PM. I actually ended up playing from eleven AM to one PM and then from two to four—the same amount of time that was agreed upon in the contract, just delayed by one hour. The client was happy and I was grateful that they were nice enough to work with me in such a stressful situation.

I made a few errors and caused this mistake to happen. First, I broke protocol and did not bring in all my gear the night before. I brought my guitar in, but not my amp and pedal board. I usually bring all three of them in every night. I had two gigs the day before and got home pretty late that night—around two AM. My reasoning at the time was, I'll just bring in my guitar so I have less to do in the morning. But when I woke up, I thought I had left all of my gear, guitar included, in the van so I could just hop in and drive to the morning gig. I didn't double-check. I didn't look in the hall closet where I store my guitar. I just woke up really tired, got dressed, hopped in the van, and took off to the airport. I am always learning from my mistakes and this one made me go back over my rules of protocol. I had to have a good laugh at myself and move on. We all make mistakes sometimes and it's how we deal with them that matters.

BROKEN MIXER

I arrived at a gig a few years ago, loaded in, set up, and went to the bar to eat a salad. When it was time to start playing, I went to the stage, tuned up, turned off the house music, and started to play. Only nothing was coming out of my PA. I remained calm and ran a dummy check to make sure everything was plugged in and turned on and all the dials were set where they were supposed to be. Everything appeared fine, but no sound was coming out of my microphone or my guitar. I happened to touch the top of my mixer, and it was really hot. I knew right away that had to be the problem.

I left the stage to find a manager. I explained the situation to him and called the local music store to see if they had a mixer on hand for me to buy. They did, and I asked them to have it waiting at the counter for me so I could pop in and pop right back out. I told the restaurant manager I would be back as soon as I could, and off I went.

When I returned to the restaurant, I pulled the mixer out of the box and went back to the stage. I did a quick switch-out and plugged in all my cables. Everything went back to normal and I played a great show. I started about forty-five minutes late and I played an extra-long first set to make up for some of the delay. It wasn't a big deal to the client, because I had been working with them for about four years. I knew all the employees and was friends with the management team, so they were all very understanding and supportive. I don't even want to think about how things would have gone if it was my first gig at a new client's venue. I was lucky in that regard.

Once again, I kept my cool and solved the problem as quickly as I could, and everything worked out at the end of the night.

DOUBLE BOOKING

This one happens way more often than I would like to admit. Unfortunately, as a musician working in mostly bar and restaurant environments, I am at the bottom of the list of importance. There are a lot of things going on in bars and restaurants and I get lost in the shuffle sometimes. What I mean is that sometimes the owner or manager will be forget-ful with their calendar, and accidentally book two different acts on the same day and at the same time. They have a lot of responsibilities and distractions. So every now and then, a mistake is made.

I actually find it kind of funny when I show up and another musician I know is there setting up. We have a laugh and catch up with some nice conversation. I never get upset when this happens. I just go with the flow and deal with the accidental double booking. Sometimes the manager or owner will feel badly about messing up, and compensate me somehow. That means they might pay me in full (very rare), pay me half (still rare), or feed me dinner and grab their calendar to book some more dates. I stay pretty busy and will just do something else with my unexpected night off.

As before, when dealing with adversity and a problem at a gig, I stay calm, go with the flow, show respect, and make a good business decision for my future employment with the venue. I will look back through any text messages or emails just to confirm that I had the right information. It usually boils down to a miscommunication and someone forgetting to update their calendar.

"When things go wrong, don't go with them."
—Elvis Presley

BROKEN GUITAR

I was booked to play a private party at someone's home and I went through my normal load-in and setup routine. When I started to play, something was wrong with my guitar.

I came to the conclusion that the input was broken. I was a ten-minute drive from my house, so I informed the client of the situation and went home to get my backup guitar. When I returned to the party, I put on a new pack of strings and started playing about five minutes after the agreed-upon start time. I made up for the delay by playing ten minutes past the agreed-upon stop time.

I was lucky to be so close to home when this happened. I have often thought about what I could have done if I had been farther away. The best idea I came up with was to ask the catering employees, the client, and/or the guests (who included neighbors) if anyone had a guitar I could use. I don't know if it would have worked but it would have been worth a shot.

UNEXPECTED CLOSINGS

Throughout the year I will play five to six days a week, which means I will work 260 to 312 days a year. There will be a certain number of cancellations in that time due to weather, establishments closing, or illness. Venues close for many reasons, sometimes temporarily and sometimes for good.

Sometimes they want to make renovations to improve their business. I am currently on hiatus for two months from my every-other-Tuesday gig because they are renovating the whole place. I still have plenty of gigs on my calendar. I have stopped in to say hi and check out the improvements. Our stage area is on the front porch. It has a roof and flaps to pull down when it rains, but it was often hot or cold because it was basically outside. The porch is being closed in and we will enjoy a climate-controlled stage area when they are done. I think all the other musicians who play there will appreciate the changes.

Other times, things aren't going well and the establishment is going out of business. I was playing one place every Wednesday for a couple of years just outside the Beltway in Baltimore. One Wednesday evening when I showed up to load in, I found the doors locked and nobody there. I called the owner and the manager, neither of whom answered, so I called the bartender who usually worked with me on Wednesdays. She told me that when she had showed up the night before, the door was locked and that nobody was answering her calls either. We didn't officially hear anything for more than a week. But the story we heard was that the owners were fighting over money and the place closed up. They didn't give me or the employees any notice; we were all just out of work. So I hit the streets and went out to find a new Wednesday-night gig.

WASPS

I am not a big fan of wasps; a few childhood experiences made a big impression on me and gave me a healthy respect for bees and wasps. I really try to avoid them and mind my own business. It may seem silly to some people, but I am sure someone with a sting allergy will understand what I am talking about.

About ten years ago, I was playing a gig in Tarpon Springs, Florida. I was set up on a wooden stage, and when I began playing, the wasps who were living somewhere under me came out to investigate. As soon as I would start a song, multiple wasps would start flying around me and my speakers. I believe they were triggered by the vibrations. They were even landing on my guitar neck and headstock. I would stop playing and they would go away. It was freaking me out and was a huge distraction while I was trying to perform.

On top of the fact that there were wasps living in the stage, there was no roof and I was standing in the hot sun. It was also far away from the people in the bar area who wanted to hear me play. The place did have a shaded area nearer the bar, and I was able to convince the manager to let me move there and be closer to the bar patrons. This was a win for everybody involved, and is now the place where every musician who plays there sets up.

A few years ago I was playing a gig in Port Richey, Florida. I was standing in the stage area and was five or six songs into my first set. I had noticed a few wasps flying by, but it was no big deal. As I started a happy reggae song I like to play, I noticed that there were more wasps and they were flying really close to my head. I'm about six-two and the stage had a low roof. I looked up to see a wasps' nest about a foot above my head.

I slowly stepped on my tuner pedal to mute my guitar, unplugged it, and slowly walked out of the stage area. I found one of the barbacks and explained that I had sting allergies and needed someone to spray and knock down the nest. This kid was about six-six and had long arms so he grabbed a can of spray, headed towards the nest, reached out from some distance and killed them all. Afterwards he knocked down the nest and we cleared away the dead wasps. I was finally able to concentrate on my music and get back to playing the gig.

About a year ago, I was at a steady gig down the street from my house. I had been playing there for about six years and had been on their stage many times. The cover had come off of one of the electrical outlets. This particular outlet was at head level on the wall behind me and off my right shoulder. On this fine Florida evening, something was new about the situation as a wasp was continually coming and going from the outlet. It was flying past me repeatedly, only inches from my microphone and my face.

I was struggling with my fear, and it was very distracting, so I stopped and found a manager. He grabbed some spray and sprayed the area all around the outlet. When the wasp left again and flew away, I quickly duct-taped the outlet shut. When the wasp came back, it could not get in and explored the taped-over area. Eventually it left and never came back.

One more example of this happened just a few weeks ago, at a new venue for me. While I was setting up I didn't notice anything out of the ordinary. I had played the place once before, and it rained like crazy, but everything stayed dry and there were no leaks. The roof covered enough space that the wind didn't blow the rain in on me. So I had confidence in everything going well, even with the chance of a thunderstorm.

This comfort completely vanished as I started playing. A steady stream of wasps flew by me, over and over again. It really was happening about every minute or so, and sometimes there were two at once. I knew that they would go home around sunset, but on that day sunset was about 8:30 PM. I started at six PM. I was going to have to be patient and stand firm as wasps continuously flew past my knees, my torso, and my microphone. I had evidently set up directly in these little guys' flight path. It was a true test of concentration, as well as overcoming fear and severe distraction.

At any moment on a gig, a variable can pop up and make me call an audible. I try to be prepared for anything I can think of, but life has a funny way of throwing us curve balls. I wish you all the success on your gigs and watch out for the occasional wasps' nest. They are definitely interested in our sounds and vibrations.

9/11, RECESSION, HURRICANE IRMA

"Musicians want to be the loud voice
for so many quiet hearts."
—Billy Joel

I think everyone remembers where they were when the 9/11 attacks happened. I was at home and was just waking up when my phone started ringing repeatedly. A little bit later I was sitting on the couch and watching TV when the second plane hit the second tower. I am not going to recall all the rest that happened that day. I am sure we all have our own memories of where we were and how traumatic it was for our country.

The reason I am including this story in the book is because I was not prepared to be in an emergency situation financially. What happened after the horrible day of 9/11 was a complete work stoppage for me for months. Nobody was going out to bars for fun or live music. Most people were staying at home watching TV to see what was happening. Everyone was anticipating our country going to war. The places I was playing at the time had to cancel all live music. With no customers in their bars, they couldn't afford to keep spending money on solo acts or bands. It took a while for me to dig out of the financial hole I found myself in, but it was a learning experience.

Another example of a tough time to be a SAM playing music for a living was during the 2009 recession. I was once again caught off guard and not financially prepared. This situation was by no means as drastic as the 9/11 events. Mostly bars cut back on the amount of days they had live music or lowered the pay for music acts. People weren't going out as much. I had just moved to Florida, and tourism really took a hit that year. I had to lean on some credit cards and later dig myself out of debt over time. It actually lasted more than a year, and the venues took a while to bounce back from their losses as well.

Another time that I was tested by a situation that was completely out of my control was just a couple of years ago, when Hurricane Irma hit Florida. My home was fine and I was safe but the power was knocked out for more than a week in lots of places. So once again bars, restaurants, and venues had to cut live music from the budget. It's hard to set up a PA system and play when there is no electricity.

I look back on these scenarios as financial emergency situations for me. I was blessed to still have food, housing, a car, and my health. But work was hard to find and the money was slow to come in. I have learned to manage my money better when things are going well. When I am busy, with lots of gigs on the books, I will plan ahead for situations like these just in case something happens.

MIC DROP

I have been a Solo Acoustic Musician for a very long time, and I still get surprised by new things that happen on the job. Recently, I was playing a construction business's thirtieth anniversary party. That was quite an accomplishment and these people were ready to party. The company was run by a husband-and-wife team who hired a caterer, a bartender, and a big tent company to provide their employees with an awesome night of thanks for all their hard work.

When I arrive at a private party, I go through my list and ask my usual questions. Then I ask if they will need a microphone to make a speech or an announcement. I was told that the owner would like to talk to the crowd after the food service. I set aside an extra mic for the man to use and told him to let me know between songs when he wanted to talk. As he started talking, I stepped to the side and walked to the back of the tent to make sure he was loud enough. Then I returned to the side of the stage and waited for him to be done.

As he seemed to be winding down his speech, I tried to make eye contact and let him know I was right there to hand the mic off to. This is when a thing I'd never seen before happened. He lifted his arm above his head and just dropped my microphone to the ground! This caused a burst of feedback and I scrambled to turn off the channel and amp as quickly as I could. This was very unexpected and shocking to me. I unplugged that mic and went back to playing music.

At the end of the evening, when I was loading out, the wife/owner came to find me and give me a fifty-dollar tip. She also asked me if my microphone was OK, to which I replied, No, it is not OK. It didn't have a dent on the outside, but what concerned me was the possibility of the fine-tuned mechanisms on the inside having problems after being dropped more than six feet to the ground. She offered to pay for the mic and a couple of weeks later she sent me a check for $100 to replace it.

It paid off to keep my cool and stay as professional as possible. There was a lot of drinking going on at that party, and I did not want to confront anybody about my microphone that night. I was actually going to wait and follow up with them on Monday. Since she brought it up with me, I went ahead and made arrangements with her at the end of the party. It all worked out great and I hope I get to play music at their next company event.

In summation, things can go wrong and stuff will happen. As long as I stay calm, try to problem-solve, and act professionally, I will be fine at the end of the day regardless of how the situation ends. I keep insurance in case of a major accident of some kind. Having it gives me a little bit of peace of mind. I keep my insurance certificate in the glove box of my van so that it is always on the gig with me and I suggest that you do the same. Hopefully all of your gigs go well and you don't encounter any of the problems that I have, but just in case I hope you get prepared for them. Keep your head up and be safe out there.

LOSING A CLIENT

I don't like to lose clients, but sometimes it's beyond my control. Here are a couple of examples of how this can happen. I am still working on repairing the relationships and playing these places again. I will stay persistent and professional in how I conduct my business so that I may be able to rebuild those bridges.

I arrived at a brewery in St. Petersburg, Florida, and walked into the warehouse where the stage was, where a nine-piece band was already setting up. I was confused; I knew I was at the right place and at the right time according to my calendar. I went into the taproom to find the manager who had booked me. I was instructed to wait for her to come down. So I waited. When she finally came to the bar area to talk to me, she just shook her head and told me today was their Oktoberfest. Now, mind you, it was the last weekend of September that year.

I took out my phone and looked up our email interaction, showing her clearly that on May 23 she had offered me the date and time, to which I agreed, and we had both confirmed the information in the email. She didn't know what to do, and didn't apologize. All she did was ask me to please wait, and then she left. A little while later, another manager handed me a check for $100 to compensate me for my time. This was not the full amount, but I considered it at least something for my time and left.

The part that wasn't cool to me was that I had liked playing there the first two times, and they had seemed to genuinely like my music. It has been two years now and I have not played there again. The manager is still working there and still handling the booking. The problem is, she isn't responding to my emails or follow-up phone calls. The situation is out of my control. I didn't do anything wrong, but I am losing a client because of someone else's mistake.

A similar example of this situation occurred at another brewery in Sarasota, Florida. The employee who was handling the calendar booked me through email. Once again, it's important to always confirm bookings via email or text message. I drove an hour from home each way, set up on time, played great, and had a fun show this particular day.

After I packed up and loaded out, I went into the taproom to get paid. A bartender went to the office and came back with an envelope. I opened it up and saw that the check was written for half of the agreed amount. I asked the bartender for the manager or owner and was told that neither of them were there. Evidently they had left for the day before my last set. Frustrated, I drove home knowing I would have to follow up on this later. There was nothing I could do at the moment.

The following day I was on the phone in the afternoon to the brewery and I spoke with the owner. She informed me that the manager had a contract with me for the smaller amount of money. So our conversation was interesting, because I explained to her that I did not have or sign any contract for this gig. I did, however, have an email confirmation and I told her that I would gladly forward it to her if she would give me her email address.

Once I sent her the email, she assured me that she would send the other half of my money and apologized. A week went by and I followed up with another phone call. I was fortunate again to get the owner on the phone, and she apologized for forgetting to send the check. A few days later I received a check with a note offering another apology. She also explained that the woman who had been handling the calendar was no longer working there, because of even more mistakes at the brewery.

Although I didn't make a mistake or cause the problem, I have not played there again. I have emailed and called trying to book more gigs, only to be ignored. It has been about a year and I am still hoping to get back in at that particular brewery. They have a big stage and an awesome beer garden.

These were unfortunate situations where I had to stand up for myself and point out the fact that someone else was wrong. The disappointment is multiplied by losing a client and therefore the gigs and the money on my calendar. My calendar is full and I am gigging steadily, but I still don't like to lose clients because of miscommunications like these. I don't think I can offer a lesson on how to fix this type of situation. I can only keep trying to book another gig with these clients. I usually wait a little while between sending emails, and hope that I can then mend the bridge or that someone new is booking their calendar.

 **BE A PRO**

---

*"Learn the rules like a pro, so you can
break them like an artist."*
—Pablo Picasso

Professionals like order. What I mean by this is that any pro
will tell you that they have organized their world and will not
tolerate disorder. In order to do a good job on my gigs I like
to have a plan, a system, and an organized pattern of events.
This will ensure that even though there may be variables like
hecklers which I have a plan to deal with, my gig will go pretty
much as planned. By being organized and having a plan, a pro
can adapt to tough situations and still perform at a top level.

In the face of fear, a professional will have the tools to
adapt and conquer that which an amateur cannot. A pro
knows that being in the moment with focus on the task at
hand will make fear recede into the background. There will
be random challenges that can distract a SAM in the middle
of a gig, while playing a song, or when you are on a break.
Fear not. Staying calm and sticking to the plan will see you
through to the result you desire.

Hecklers and random rainstorms don't care what kind of
a day I am having. I could be on cloud nine, feeling good, and

something or someone can come out of nowhere and try to rain on my parade. I could unintentionally break a string, a baby could cry and scream uncontrollably, or a person can interrupt me during a very technical and difficult guitar solo to request a song that I don't know or even like. I am prepared for this, and it will not ruin my day or affect me at all. I will continue my gig that day and be in front of a different group of strangers tomorrow. Being prepared for every situation I can think of has helped me through quite a few situations that I wasn't aware of or prepared for.

Asking for help is another trait that professionals share. I do not let my ego get in the way of being humble and asking for help. Maybe it's a guitar technique I am struggling to grasp—a certain style of rhythm or just a basic scale that I can't seem to figure out. I know plenty of amazing guitar players I can ask to help me. It usually helps to have an extra perspective and a different approach to a task that I am struggling with. I don't know everything and some things I can't figure out on my own. In music, as in any part of life, learning is never-ending.

A professional is patient. The results of your dedication will appear to you over time. There is really no way to rush to the finish line in this marathon of life. I think there are many reasons why pros are so calm, but one is that they know the difference between their strengths and weaknesses. This one thing saves a lot of time and struggles that amateurs go through.

When you recognize that you are not good at something on the job, you can decide to stop doing it. You can practice more, or figure out a way to make it with the skills you have and stop trying to do something you are not good at. I can't sing certain high notes in certain songs, so I don't. I sing them in key and in my range. This works out a lot better than straining to hit a note and then going flat as well as hurting myself. I cringe sometimes when I am out at a bar and hear someone try for a note that they clearly cannot hit. I learned a long time ago to do what I can and to try not to embarrass myself in front of the audience. Part of the process of being a pro is to look at yourself as an employee. I have learned what I am capable of and what I should not attempt on stage.

On the other hand, I know my strengths. When I figure out that I am good at something, I like to focus on it for a while and make sure that I showcase it at gigs. Maybe it's a new guitar technique. Maybe it's the way I sound like a famous artist when I am singing. Either way, when I find a strength in my abilities I will incorporate it and know that I am good at it. This will always help me to have direction and confidence in what I am doing. It will not matter what the situation is, where I am, or what is happening around me because I will know I am presenting the best version of myself to the audience.

Professionals and amateurs have different attitudes about how they conduct themselves. A professional knows to expect to be miserable. Not everybody in the audience is going to like what you do and we as SAMs are leaving ourselves open to their judgments. I have had to deal with hecklers that didn't like what I was doing and still I smiled and played through the "pain." Some people think that being a pro is getting paid for what you do. But it is more than that. It means dealing with adversity in a way that is graceful, humble, and kind.

"We're musicians. We make music for a living.
It's that simple. Nothing else matters."
—Eddie Van Halen

A professional does it for the love of the game and enjoys the work it takes to become really good at the task. Have you ever noticed that greats like Tiger Woods, Kobe Bryant, and Michael Jordan kept wanting to learn? Did you ever think that the best musicians would just stop practicing and think they know it all? My grandmother used to tell me that a great violin player can take a day off of practice and nobody notices. That same player can take another day off of practice and only he/she notices. But if that player takes off another day of practice, then the whole world notices. You have to strive to learn and become better at everything you can. Practice your skills and apply your newfound knowledge to your vocation of being the best Solo Acoustic Musician you can be.

Being a pro at anything takes time and energy. You have to have focus on what you want to achieve. What is your goal? Do you want to play songs at an open mic? Do you want to become better at playing in front of people? Do you want to play a "gig" once in a while where your friends and family can come hear you play and sing in a bar? Do you want to play your guitar, sing, and make a living with your music by doing gigs at bars, restaurants, and special events or private parties? Just like any other job, you have to decide what it is that you want to do.

The basic goal of this book is to help you become a pro. There is a lot of information in all these chapters but you have to choose what you will use. I know some of you will have played gigs and think that you already have it figured out. I am here to tell you that I have often felt that way. It's unfortunate, but I am still learning things about my job, and we are in a world of constant change. Variable change is an equation that I most equate to playing blackjack. I never know what's going to happen at a gig, but I can control what I do before, on, and after the gig.

I know that some people who read this book are serious pros. I also know that quite a few of them will see something new in this book, or a reminder of something they haven't thought about or encountered for a long time. As any good pro knows, a reminder of a challenging situation or a simple challenge to remember a situation that they went through is always welcome. It can show up on the job the next day and you might say to yourself, "I just read that in a book." I am purposely filling this book with a lot of information that can affect all levels of musicians. Yes, it is geared towards Solo Acoustic Musicians, but I am sure you have gathered by now that the information can be applied to a lot more than that.

WARDROBE

You have to be comfortable and wear what works for you, of course... right? Well, as you will find out when this is how you make your living, you may have to follow some rules about your wardrobe. A tiki bar gig by the ocean may be very casual, while a corporate function in the city may require dress clothes. I know it is a no-brainer but it still has to be addressed.

My favorite casual attire is shorts, a T-shirt, and tennis shoes. I keep a small range of dress clothes available for those occasions that require it. Every situation is different, and being able to be flexible and go with the flow is important.

I recently played a VIP party for the owner and select fans of the Tampa Bay Lightning hockey team here in Tampa. I was given a team polo shirt to wear for the gig. Pretty good swag! I have also worked with the Toronto Blue Jays, the Philadelphia Phillies, and the Tampa Bay Buccaneers. It's awesome when they hook me up with a hat and jersey to wear during the gig! Of course, then I wear them around town and support the teams. I try to keep my wardrobe concerns minimal and basic. I have everything I need to cover every occasion, and get blessed with some special event prizes too.

CONFIDENCE

As an artist or as anyone in life for that matter, we will deal with criticism. Getting on stage in front of a room full of people takes a certain amount of guts. It can actually be quite nerve-wracking to be a public speaker. Public speaking is known to be an even less desirable thing to do than going to the dentist. But when a person gives a speech, they are on stage for maybe twenty minutes at the most, and that's a long speech. Also, they only do this once in a while. I have to stand up in front of a crowd of twenty or thirty to hundreds of random, possibly unsupportive people, four to six times a week. To become a good Solo Acoustic Musician, you will have to overcome the fear of being on stage in front of strangers and learn to embrace the challenge of entertaining them.

Even once you have had experience on stage, or in the corner of the room where you set up and play, a little bit of nervousness can creep in. I have to be confident that I know what I am doing. I know what I want to do. I know that I have the skills necessary to play and sing at a high level. Everyone will have self-doubt in a number of situations. Experience and preparation bring a sense of confidence.

DON'T TEXT ON STAGE

I was on break at a gig the other night in a new bar down at the beach near my home. It was my second time playing there. I was getting a refill of my water when the manager on duty came over to talk to me. He was sharing some compliments with me about what he liked that I was doing. He thought it was great that I was engaging the crowd and interacting with the audience. He then confided in me that none of the other musicians who had played there in the last month had done that at all. He told me that some of the other people who had played there had just stood in the corner and played songs. He was hoping they would have more presence in the room.

As the conversation continued, I asked him if my volume was good and told him to let me know how it was throughout the night. I explained that I like to get to know the managers at new venues I play, and added that we have to learn to work together so all of us make money.

His response was a story about a musician who had played there a week before. He told me that he walked out of the kitchen to see the musician standing in the corner texting with both hands. He explained that the musician had set a loop or was playing a track and was just standing there texting on his phone instead of performing the song. He said that the musician looked like a deer in the headlights and scrambled to put his phone down when he was spotted. The manager then walked over and told him to pack up because he was done for the night. He added that he later emailed the third party agent and requested that she not book that musician at his location anymore.

So there it is, folks. Do not stand on stage or in the corner where you are playing and text people on your phone during a song or your set time.

TRACKING

Tracking is not a new concept and it could already be part of your approach to other parts of your life. When people go on a diet, they track their caloric intake. When people go to the gym, they track their weights, reps, and sets. A casino tracks every bit of data on every machine and table as well as every player with a casino card. A bar or restaurant will track every bit of food, alcohol, and expense they have. I believe that every successful business is tracking data and statistics to make improvements that will lead to greater profits and a better experience for the customer.

---

*You can't stay the same. If you're a musician and a
singer, you have to change, that's the way it works.*
—Van Morrison

Several years ago I started to do some tracking of my own. I make a note on my calendar of how much money in tips I make every night. At the end of the month I will add them all up for a total tip amount for the month. Then I will divide that total by the number of gigs I did that month for a per-gig average. At the end of the year I do this again with all of the monthly totals. By collecting this data I can start to see where I need to improve or if any of my new ideas are working. It helps to give me perspective on how much extra money I make in tips. One thing that I find fun to do is to collect all my tips for the month and apply those funds to a big bill. Maybe a credit card, a car payment, or even the rent. I make it into a game for myself. Maybe you can set aside your tip money for a few months to save for a vacation.

Tracking your statistics will help you see trends in your business. What are the busiest months? Are there slow months? Is it because of tourist seasons? Are the results based on weather? If you can clearly see the number of gigs you have played, the number of cancellations you have had, and all your other totals, then you can spot deficiencies in certain areas and try to make improvements. I will strive to make sure my calendar is balanced between indoor and outdoor gigs, especially in the summer rainy season here in Florida. Keeping track of what I do is another way to get better at being a SAM.

SOLO ACOUSTIC MUSICIAN
CODE OF CONDUCT

Always be on time.

Dress appropriately for the gig.

Don't get drunk on the stage or in the venue.

Clean up after yourself at the end of your gig.

Promote your music and your gigs.

Network with other musicians.

Use your gifts and talents to help others.

Show respect to yourself and others by not engaging in lewd language on the microphone.

Represent yourself, the agents, and the clients as best you can by being professional on the gig.

 # LIFE STORIES OF A SAM

TORONTO BLUE JAYS GIG

The Toronto Blue Jays come down to Florida for their annual spring training. They also have a Florida Summer League team here that is one of their developmental farm teams. I had played several events during the summer league events throughout a two-year period beginning in 2012. Then in 2014, I was asked to play music out by the front gate before the spring training home games. My requirements were a parking spot right next to my equipment, a small tent for cover, a hot dog, a soda pop, and a bottle of water. They paid me very well and gave me half up front and half on the last day of the engagement. I played fourteen home games for them that year.

I would arrive at 10:30 AM and set up. I played until one PM, right before the national anthem that started at about 1:05 PM. After I packed up my gear and put it all into my van, I would use my lanyard, which gave me access all over the stadium, to find an open seat and watch a few innings. I actually was privileged enough to get to see Derek Jeter's last spring training game of his career. Now, I am not a big Yankees fan, but it was still pretty cool to see him play in a smaller, more intimate setting.

The one game that I watched all the innings of was when the Red Sox came to play. I have some friends from up north who visit from the first week of January until late April or early May every year. Down here we call the people who do this "snowbirds." I made a request for three tickets to the Red Sox game and was given three seats in the second row behind home plate. My friends came to see me by the gate and I gave them their tickets. After I was done with my set, I joined them in the stadium to watch the game. This couple is retired and grew up in Massachusetts, and the Red Sox are still their favorite team. The Red Sox decisively won the final game on October 30, becoming the World Series champions for 2013, and it was awesome for my friends to get to see their big league baseball stars up so close.

I was also given some Blue Jays gear to wear. An official jersey, some shirts, a hat, and a koozie. I asked for a wristband but they were out of stock in the gift shop at the time. I still have all the swag from this experience and wear it around town sometimes.

RICHMOND, VA

I went on a road trip from Baltimore to North Carolina and back for gigs. I was on my way home and stopped in Richmond, Virginia, to play a gig for door money. It was a gamble, but it was only a couple hours from home and it filled out my mini tour calendar for one last show. I was getting a bad vibe from the owner all night. She was just rude and not a happy person. I did get along with the doorman, though, and that proved to be more important for me at the end of the night.

I had about ten minutes left in the show when lightning struck the telephone pole on the corner right outside the bar. I was playing on a small stage with a big front window as my backdrop. That lightning strike was very close to where I was standing, and even closer to the bouncer standing right in the doorway. Then the power went out, immediately after the lightning hit the pole. This put an end to my set, and I also had to break down in the dark.

It was a five-dollar cover charge that night and about sixty-three people paid. The doorman confided in me that he let a few of his friends in for free and that the owner had done the same thing. He then handed me $315 because he thought the owner would stiff me and not give me any money. He mentioned that she had done that to travelling musicians before, and then he left. I packed up as quickly as I could and got out of there. Was the lightning an omen? I don't know and I don't care—I am just thankful that the guy working the door was nice enough to do the right thing by me. I never played that place again!

PHIL'S GRILL, VIRGINIA BEACH, VA

Phil's Grill used to be a cool place to play on Eleventh Street between Atlantic and Pacific Avenues. This place had great food with dreadlocked hippies cooking and serving. There was a large mural of famous dead musicians including Jerry Garcia, Jimi Hendrix, Keith Moon, and Sid Vicious behind me where I would set up. Unfortunately, Phil's is no longer there.

One night after playing my gig at Phil's I was joined by some friends back at the hotel. It was a cold winter night in Virginia. We stayed up late, put on our sweaters and coats, and took blankets out onto the pool deck to use the pool lounge chairs. Then we laid out at about three in the morning and watched a meteor shower.

WATKINS GLEN, NY

There is a little town called Watkins Glen in upstate New York and I used to go there a few times a year to play. Watkins Glen is at the southernmost point of one of the Finger Lakes. This lake isn't very wide but it is about seventeen miles long up both sides. I never actually drove up and around it. Watkins Glen also has another major attraction besides the lake: at the top of the mountain, and south of town is a NASCAR racetrack.

The bar I played in had a little stage in the corner that was about a foot tall. This allowed me to see over the top of the crowd. The owners were two young guys fresh out of college, starting their first business together. This place was a popular late-night spot for the young party crowd. When I arrived to load in and set up, I would bring my cooler in from the van so I could load it up with bottled water, cans of beer, and a bottle of cheap whiskey. I would line up small plastic cups along the front of the stage to give away the cheap whiskey to people who were paying attention to the music.

The bar would get so busy and packed that it would be four to five people deep at the bar trying to get a drink. I didn't have to fight the people to get a beer when I was on break because I had my cooler on stage. I convinced the owner to do this because I explained I only take a short break and need to get a drink. Whether it was water, a soda, or a beer, I would be taking the bartender's attention away from the paying customers and because it was going to be so busy, it could very well take my whole break to refill my beverage. On my break, there are other things I need to do besides bother the bartenders for a drink. I want to make fans and get email addresses, use the bathroom, catch my breath, and relax a little. There are several places I play currently where I will get my own water or tea so as to not bother the bar staff.

This gig was a lot of fun every time and it also had a couple perks that made it worth the long drive up to New York from Baltimore, where I was living at that time. One of the owners had an older brother who was the cop on duty when I was done playing my show. This meant that I didn't have to worry about being hassled by the police at three in the morning when I was leaving. The other perk was that the mother of the other owner owned a little motel one mile up the west side of the lake and would give me a room to stay in for the weekend. It was a great setup for me!

OBSERVING THE ROOM

After many years of working as a Solo Acoustic Musician I have logged thousands of hours on the stage. I have been observing the room for a really long time. It's actually quite fun if you are into people-watching. I grew up watching people at the beach and on the boardwalk in Ocean City, Maryland. I think I have actually grown some skills by paying attention to the audience.

After many years of loud music and people trying to talk to me or make a request while I am still playing a song, I believe that I am pretty decent at reading lips now. Another thing I believe I have learned is how to read the body language of people in the audience. I can tell when a couple is happy or fighting, which is actually one of the easiest things to figure out.

In this day and age of internet dating sites and first meets at bars and restaurants, I can almost always tell when two people are meeting for a first date. It is actually quite entertaining to watch. I can tell right away which person is more into the other. A few years ago I started sharing my insights with some of the bartenders I work with and pointing out what I perceived as first-date encounters. It's kind of a fun game I play with employees of places I play; I like to see if they agree with my assessment of the situation.

Most of the time it is fun to watch people in a crowd. But every now and then something crazy happens—maybe a fight will break out or someone will have a medical emergency like a heart attack or a stroke. Either way, I am an observer of life on my gigs and here are a few stories of things I saw happen.

One night in a small town on the Virginia coastline I was playing a bar on the second floor of a building. It was a late show and the crowd was pretty rowdy and drinking heavily. I actually had people on the dance floor in front of me. Halfway through one of my songs, I saw a guy leave the bathroom and walk across the dance floor toward his table right in front of me. I happened to notice that he had peed his pants! I made eye contact with him and grinned, to acknowledge that I saw what had happened. He then walked very fast to his chair. About two songs later, he was on the dance floor with a woman for a slow song. They were grinding each other pretty hard and I just had to laugh...

In another small town on the eastern shore of Maryland I was playing a restaurant on a river, down a country road, and quite a way out in the boonies. A man was drinking there and had become very intoxicated. He was asked to leave and was led outside. All of a sudden, there was a commotion near the front door. The man who was asked to leave had been outside for about ten minutes and wanted to come back in. As the bartender was calling for a manager to help, the rest of us started to piece together what was going on. The man was covered in his own fecal matter! Somehow, they convinced him to sit on the waiting bench on the front porch of the bar. It didn't take long for some Maryland State Police cars to arrive on the scene. The officers put on plastic gloves, opened the trunk of their cruiser, and pulled out a big roll of clear plastic. They got the guy to lay down so they could roll him up in the plastic and get him into the backseat of the car. Everyone there was in shock!

I have been living in the Tampa Bay area for more than a decade now, and I have made lots of friends among the managers and owners of local bars and restaurants. One evening when I was in the middle of my last song, at almost ten o'clock, I saw a man push a female manager to the ground and start throwing punches at the owner, who is also female. I immediately stepped on my tuner pedal to mute my guitar, unplugged it, and dropped it to the floor leaning against the wall. Then I ran across the room and grabbed the man! I lifted him off the ground and took him out the front door. I threw him on the ground and told him to get out! That's a pretty crazy thing to have happen on a gig. After cooling down and packing up, I apologized to the owner for putting my hands on someone in her place of business. She was thankful that I had removed the man and didn't take it any further. It still makes my adrenaline pump a little to this day when I think about it...

I will always be an observer and watch people as they interact at my gigs. There are lots of "normal" days and there are a few "abnormal" days here and there. Most of the time people are happy and enjoying each other's company while I play happy songs for them. But every now and then, I get a story to tell to my friends and family about a very "odd" day at work.

STAGE FRIGHT

"In my opinion, the only way to conquer stage fright is to get up on stage and play. Every time you play another show, it gets better and better."
—*Taylor Swift*

Have you ever been to a really popular open mic? Maybe one that is being hosted in a really nice listening room venue with a stage, soundman, well-equipped house sound system, and lights shining down on the stage, plus a full kitchen and bar to accommodate about one hundred patrons. This will attract lots of good musicians. I used to go to one on Tuesday nights.

I couldn't understand it the first few times I went to this particular spot. I was getting really nervous and having some stage fright–type issues. Shaky hands, sweat rolling down my forehead, and a dry throat: it got so bad that some nights I decided to take a break from playing when I went there. I would still go, buy some food and a beer, and clap for the other performers, and support the local businesses and musicians.

I didn't really understand what was going on until I saw it happen to another good musician on that stage and we got to talking. We both played out for a living and didn't get nervous at our normal bar gigs. We came to the realization that most of the time we were just background music in a restaurant where it seemed that no one was paying us much attention. So when we got on stage at this listening room and everyone was watching us and being extremely quiet, it hit us like a wave and we got nervous. On top of all that, all the quiet people paying attention to us while we were playing our original songs were really good, well-respected musicians themselves. A room full of excellent musicians watching us like hawks scared the crap out of us!

I was gigging six days a week at the time. I would use this as the excuse—that it was my night off and I didn't want to sing. I did want to support the other local musicians and the awesome venue and scene that was being created. I would show up and not bring my guitar. The owner and the bartender would both offer their guitars for me to use. I would decline week after week until finally, I told them this... "Every great masseuse loves a back rub and every great chef loves a nice meal cooked for them. I really do enjoy coming down here to listen to some good musicians and songwriters play their original music."

---

*Playing music is a beautiful thing. But
listening to music is just as great.*
—Flea

After a couple of months of hanging out on Tuesdays and not playing, I showed up with my guitar and played some of my songs. I didn't get nervous at all! I think part of it was the fact that I was used to the room and the people who came out on a regular basis. I was more comfortable in the environment and with the format of the open mic. For a few months, I was third on the list every week and I didn't get nervous there anymore. I rarely get nervous when I get up to play music in front of people, but that was a major learning experience for me.

CAR IN THE POOL

One day I showed up to a yacht and country club on a river complete with boats moored along the water's edge. It was early afternoon and people were coming out for lunch, and a small crowd was gathering around the pool. The last time I was there, the pool was under construction. Evidently, it was just completed two days before the weekend and all the kids were ready for it to open back up.

The fresh dirt surrounding the deck was wet from rain the night before and was easy to make an impression in. As I was walking out to see what was going on, I noticed tire tracks in the dirt. As I reached the pool deck I saw why everyone was gathered. There was a Ford Explorer parked in the brand-new pool! One man was lifting kids across the water to stand on top of the vehicle so they could have their picture taken... it was quite an interesting situation.

The story that circulated through the crowd was that a nineteen-year-old was driving late the night before, drunk and high, and ended up in the pool. Evidently it was very foggy, and the country backroad near the river is very winding and curvy. The pool probably saved his life. If it was not there, he would have gone straight over the bulkhead and dock and into a boat or the river. Either of those scenarios would have come to a much worse outcome, I am sure.

"I'M IN THE BAND"

I learned this one magical little sentence at an early age and it has always come in handy throughout my entire life. While I was parking on the sidewalk in between two high-rise buildings in downtown Baltimore to play a gig at a local brewery, a couple of police officers came up to talk to me in a rather cautious way. If I remember correctly, this was sometime shortly after 9/11 and they considered what I was doing to be strange behavior. As they put it, we just received a report of a suspicious van pulling up onto the sidewalk between two big buildings downtown.

The first thing I said to them was, "I'm in the band."

Then I opened all the doors and showed them my musical equipment. This satisfied their curiosity and they went on their way.

Another example of how often I might use this phrase is when I am playing events such as local beer festivals or holiday events for the city or county. These types of events usually have some sort of borders set up and I have to drive through the barricades to get my van parked next to the stage. The barricades are usually manned by some kind of security or volunteer. And what's the first thing I say to them? "I'm in the band."

Yet another example, pretty much the same, is when I am playing a private party in an exclusive neighborhood, a golf course, or a private resort. Some of these locations will have a guard booth that you must stop at and talk to a guard. The first thing I say is, "I'm in the band," followed by my name and where exactly on the property I am supposed to be.

The phrase "I'm in the band" has helped me out in some other ways as well. Like when I take a break and find myself headed towards the bathroom only to find a long line at the door. I will say something like, "Hey guys, I'm in the band and I only have a few minutes on break. Can I cut ahead in line?" This usually works. This wonderful phrase can also get me prime parking spots, free beer, and free food without me even asking for it. A brewery that I play about twice a year has the same two food trucks parked on site every weekend. When I check out the menu, I make sure to mention that "I'm in the band." They always tell me that they take care of the musicians and that my dinner is on them. I enjoy the generosity and usually throw some money equal to my food order in their tip can. At the same brewery, I get free beer because it's part of the deal. I don't drink on my gig there for many reasons, including that it's an hour's drive home. I do, however, get some cans to bring home. I am not a big craft beer drinker, and usually share them with my friends.

TROPICANA GIG

It was the beginning of the 2019 Major League Baseball season and I was booked to play some music at the Tropicana, home to the Tampa Bay Rays. I was emailed load-in directions, a parking lot map, and a parking pass. As I pulled up at the entrance to the lot I told the usher, "I'm in the band." The attendant waved me through and I slowly drove my van to Gate 7. Upon arrival, I was able to unload and go through a security checkpoint. The security officers needed to go through all my cases and put tags on all my gear, just like the airport does to your luggage. Then I jumped back in my van and drove out to lot number 9, which was about a ten-minute walk from Gate 7.

Gate 7 had a giant garage door for the ambulance to get into the concourse. This was the only spot on the fence to the field that was open, so that emergency crews had access to the field. This was also where a couple of EMT personnel would be on standby with a gurney in case of an emergency in the stadium. They had access to the field through a door in the fence.

As I was setting up, both teams were having batting practice. I made a comment to one of the crew members that I was curious if a baseball might be hit into the gap and maybe hit me. I walked over and stood in the middle of the concourse, watching a guy take batting practice. It was only a few minutes later that a security guard yelled for everyone to look out! A ball was heading straight towards the opening and right at me, so I jogged out of the way.

Another man was walking towards the exit door when a baseball came flying through the gap. It bounced off the concrete floor and actually picked up speed. I yelled at the man to look out but he didn't seem to hear me at all. The ball must have been going more than a hundred miles an hour when it grazed his button-down shirt and tie, right before it slammed into the garage door with a loud bang. He practically jumped out of his skin. The ball rolled away so I ran over, picked it up, and went over to the man. I asked him if he was OK, and if he wanted the ball. He was relieved not to have been hit and smiled. I could see the sweat running down his temple. He gladly accepted the ball and went on his way.

When the gates opened and the concourse filled with people I played a ninety-minute set.

MONTEREY, CALIFORNIA

My little sister lived in Monterey, California, for a year and I was fortunate enough to visit her there twice. She had two jobs while she lived there. One was writing part-time for a newspaper and the other was at a winery in Carmel Valley. I could tell lots of stories about touring wineries, hiking in Big Sur, driving the coastline, eating at wonderful restaurants, and many other adventures. Our days and nights were so full that I practically needed a vacation after my vacation.

One night on my second visit to Monterey we were out at a bar that had a live band. It was a four piece with two electric guitars, bass, and drums. I wouldn't normally do this but I was talking to one of the guitar players and explained that I was in town visiting family and that my sister had not seen me play in a while, and that it sure would be a treat if I could sit in on one song. Unbelievably, he agreed to let me play and the rest of the band was all right with it too.

They were a blues based rock 'n' roll band and we played a basic twelve-bar blues song. At one point when I was taking my solo, the lead singer walked over to the amp I was plugged in to and surprised the hell out of me by turning me up a little bit. I was shocked! My first instinct was to think that he was going to turn me down, and the complete opposite happened.

The owner was also the bartender that night and she was so impressed that she offered me a gig and gave us some shots of tequila that tasted like Trix cereal.

This place even had a firepit with a nice fire in it going on out back on a chill patio overlooking Monterey Bay. We could see the fishing boats shining lights on the water to trick the squid into coming close to the surface so they could scoop them up. The restaurants at the pier there have the freshest calamari in the world.

AIRPORT GIGS

I have played in the Tampa International Airport many times. I believe these to have been some of the most fulfilling gigs that I have ever done. Travel can be very stressful and comes with hidden obstacles and challenges. I found that when I was playing happy songs and smiling at strangers passing by that I was actually making them feel good. Quite a few times I was approached and told that I had made someone's day. People would tell me how their day had gone badly, with delays, snow at home, being stuck for six hours on an extended unplanned layover, etc. An author told me she didn't have any money to tip me, but she gave me a signed copy of her book. So I grabbed one of my CDs from my guitar case and gave it to her in trade. Another lady wrote me a heartwarming note that I shared with the airport staff in charge of events. They were blown away by what they read and made copies for their bosses! I have also received pictures of me drawn by little children.

I was not allowed to solicit tips on these gigs. I did average more than $30 in tips without a tip can. My record for tips in the airport was $74! I think that's pretty impressive since I didn't have a tip can. You're also less likely to get tips when people are walking by very quickly. Many times a passer-by would reach towards their pocket for money and then ask, "Where's your tip can?" or "Why don't you have a tip can?" They would keep moving and not give me a tip.

As I've mentioned, I do keep a table next to me on my gigs for my drinks, phone, picks, cough drops or Tic-Tacs, and business cards. It also helps to block people from running into my mic stand. On an airport gig, this is important because people will be walking by very briskly and get very close. An unintended consequence of placing my table there is that people will put money on it. I retrieve the money in between songs so that I do not get in trouble for soliciting tips. I am allowed to accept them, but not ask for them. Some gigs I have played in the airport require me to go through security but this particular gig is in the main terminal, and yes, they do validate my parking!

When I do have to go through security, I have to make it through in one trip. This is one of the reasons why I downsized my gear, buying a different kind of cart and a backpack guitar case. I can get all the gear I need loaded into gigs all in one trip. It makes it easier and quicker for me, and cuts down on the time it takes to load in and set up. I can now arrive a little later to work if I want to.

A fun highlight to an already good gig at the airport was a Bono impersonator surprising me while I was playing the U2 song "I Still Haven't Found What I'm Looking For." I had my eyes closed while singing and opened them when a guy started singing with me. A guy who looked just like Bono! It was a lot of fun to play and sing a few more U2 songs with him there. As people were walking by, they were doing double takes, looking back at us and stopping to see if it was the real Bono. This experience definitely spiced up my afternoon in the airport. On my break we chatted and have stayed in touch.

NEW TO TOWN

I have moved across the country a few times and I usually hit the ground running by getting gigs as quickly as possible. But just in case I struggle with finding places to play, I like to have a contingency plan in place that I can implement quickly. I have two basic things that I have done in the past. I am always reluctant to take on any kind of job other than playing music full-time. But every now and then it doesn't hurt and may even be necessary to make rent.

The first option I have found to be good for a couple of reasons. It's a cliché that musicians have to have a "real job" or they must be delivering pizza part-time. Well, I actually did deliver pizza part-time for a few months when I was new to a particular town. It is a way to make some quick cash every shift from tips, as well as usually getting some food for free from the restaurant. Another bonus is that you will learn the five-mile radius near your new home very quickly. This can help you find places to play, and really helped me when I moved to Seattle at the age of eighteen.

The second option I have used before can be done even while delivering pizzas too. When you get to your new city, look up the local stadiums, theatres, amphitheatres, or major music venues and try to find out who is hiring the stagehands. Most major cities will have a stagehands' union. The union takes time to get into but they usually subcontract to smaller companies that need manpower constantly. I have been successful finding work with stagehand companies in Seattle and Denver. Helping unload a grand piano down a metal ramp from a Mack truck in the snow is quite the fun time...

I actually started doing stagehand work when I was in high school. Three times in my life I have leaned on this kind of work for supplemental income. It is also a fun way to get a free concert! I have had the pleasure of seeing and meeting some pretty good musicians. Even when I am working full-time and staying very busy, I like to keep my name on a list and when I get a call I can make a choice. If I happen to have the day off and I like the artist who is playing the concert, I might take the job. I will make $20 an hour and get a free concert along with it. I know it's lifting boxes and not playing music, but it is still in the music business.

I was working a concert in a beach town, at a stage right on the beach, and 10,000 Maniacs were the headlining act. Their keyboard player asked me about the location of the nearest liquor store and where he could find some live music to check out later that night. I knew some friends who were going to be playing a few blocks away from the concert and about six blocks from his hotel. They were a really good power trio and had a good sound. I told him I would be going there after work because I liked their music.

I was sitting at the bar when I felt a hand on my shoulder. As I turned around I saw four members of the band standing behind me. I told them I would only tell my friends in the band who they were and I offered to buy them a round of drinks. The keyboard player said no, he was buying. I insisted, only to have him say, "We just made $35,000 for our one-hour set and I have six platinum records under my belt. You have directed us to a cool little bar with a good band, so I am buying you a couple of drinks tonight." I accepted the offer and we all just chilled out together.

I have met several famous people while doing stagehand work, including Travis Tritt, Tim McGraw, Mark Chesnut, Chely Wright, Roy "Futureman" Wooten, Kool and the Gang, members of 10,000 Maniacs, the Power Rangers (East Coast

Members), members of Alabama, and a handful of others. I have also met sidemen hired for the tours as well as many stage construction, sound, and lighting guys. All of the headliners were nice enough to say hi, shake my hand, or sign an autograph. A few of them even had a conversation with me. I always thought of it as a privilege and honor to meet any of them at all.

DON'T SOLICIT THE FAMOUS ARTIST

As a SAM I have some CDs and promotional items as well as business cards. It is a big-time no-no to give these items to a famous person or part of their team while working on a concert. I saw a coworker give a demo CD to Kool of Kool and the Gang once. Well, evidently Kool did not appreciate his initiative and sent someone from his team to talk to our boss. Needless to say, that kid didn't ever work on our stage crew again. So just remember that if you choose to explore being a stagehand part-time, don't approach concert artists with your demos or business cards in the hopes of making a connection.

Like a tip can at a private party, the solicitation of a touring artist's interest may backfire on you. I had always hoped that one of the many concerts I worked would lead to something more, by way of making a connection in the music business. But I did not ever do anything that I thought would get me fired. Of course, if an artist wanted to talk to me or ask questions about the local area, I was allowed to interact with them. I just didn't initiate any conversations and especially not about my music. It's an unwritten code of etiquette. Stagehands don't bother the artists.

One year, when I was in my early twenties, I worked the biggest concert I have ever been a part of, the Tibetan Freedom concert in Washington, D.C. It was in the old RFK stadium and included more than fifty famous bands and artists. We had to wear mountain climbing rigging and build a giant scaffolding stage that included multiple floors and two stages. While one band was performing another was breaking down and yet another was then setting up.

I couldn't believe all the famous people I saw backstage at this two day concert. It took two days to build the stage and one to take it down. During the breakdown of the scaffolding it started raining, so we had to be extra careful not to let the pieces slip and fall onto people below. During the second afternoon of music, lightning hit a section of seating in the stadium. It was all metal so it spread under the seats and hurt about two dozen people. The concert was shut down quickly and emergency personnel responded immediately. A lot of the bands went to the 9:30 club in D.C. and did stripped-down performances, including some solo acoustic sets. People who had a ticket stub could get in for free.

I enjoyed the work and the free concerts. I was able to be backstage and supplement my income, and schedule my shifts for nights when I didn't have a gig. When I was younger, it was a lot of fun and gave me some awesome concert experiences.

Another route that I know other musicians have gone is to work at a music store or to teach lessons. I have never done either of those jobs full- or part-time, but I can see how that could work for an individual who is new to town. I can imagine that being around the music store all the time would help in networking with local musicians on all levels. That can lead to friendships and gig-sharing.

TAKE THE ROAD LESS TRAVELLED

Two roads diverged in a wood and I—I
took the one less traveled by
—Robert Frost

It's about a three-hour drive from my house in the Tampa Bay area to Gainesville, Florida, the home of the University of Florida Gators. They're a Division 1 university, which means that there are a lot of local watering holes and clubs. Several years ago, a place I had been playing for a while where I lived opened a franchise in Gainesville. After talking it over with the owners, I booked a date to play at the new location. This would be a little bit different show than what I normally do, as I was bringing two other Solo Acoustic Musicians with me. We were each going to play our own sets.

I left my house that morning and picked up the other two musicians on the way up the road to Gainesville. We decided to take back roads instead of the highway on the way there and back. We went two different ways and enjoyed the beautiful Florida countryside. After the gig, we stayed the night at one of the bartenders' apartments.

The next day, we started our return drive and took Route 20 going west. As we passed through the town of Bronson, a very small one-stoplight farming town, we noticed a rather large gravestone with a big red guitar on it. We decided to turn around and go back to the cemetery to see who it was. It was the gravesite of Bo Diddley, who was a very famous blues guitar player and rock 'n' roll pioneer. We took a few pictures and got back on our way. When we arrived home, we had a fun story to tell our other musician friends.

 **AFTERWORD**

I have had a lot of fun writing this book. The experiences I have shared are true and accurate to the best of my memory. There have been trials in the process, but I promise you that my intent is to tell you how I do it and explain this lifestyle as I see it from my point of view. I hope you have enjoyed the stories and can use the information I have shared.

There are no classes in school to become a working musician or band member, especially not a SAM. You can learn music theory or how to play an instrument, but not how to use those skills to make a living. I hope that what I have written can give you some insight into the world of a SAM: what it takes to do it, be good at it, and become a professional performer who can make a decent living by using your skills.

There were things I didn't know when I was getting into this. There were choices I made at an early age that would affect the rest of my life. It is unfair to call what I do a "job." I found out over time that it was quite a bit more than that. It started out as an obsession, turned into a job, then became a career, and ultimately became a lifestyle. It became who I was and it is a major part of my identity to this day. It has defined much of my life.

There are stories with places, dates, and times that I could put into this book but I don't think that information applies to the concept and what it is meant to teach or learn. The truth be told I don't remember every gig I have played. I certainly don't think I can list all of the places I have played over thirty years, so I won't try. I will tell you that I am very grateful for all the clients who have hired me and shown me respect. The stories are mostly ambiguous on purpose because I hope everyone can find a way to relate to my experiences. After somewhere around eight thousand gigs, it's hard to remember all the situations I have been through.

I know full-time musicians have a lot of different experiences, and I hope that some of my stories, as well as the information in this book can be useful and helpful as well as entertaining. I don't believe that this is my life story as much as it is a basic guide for those who choose to play music for a living. In any profession, the successful ones always give back and teach or coach others to achieve those same goals of chasing their passion or purpose, and fulfilling an individual dream.

Times are always changing and evolving, but I believe many of the tips, ideas, and stories in this book will stand the test of time. Although technology has given us new tools to use on our gigs, I still have to demonstrate high value by playing and singing well. My advice is to never stop trying to get better and learn more about your job, career, and lifestyle. Follow up your intentions with actions towards your goals.

While writing this book, I have been doing some reflection on how I act on a gig. After rereading the chapter on attitude, I realized that I have to practice what I preach! I found myself really smiling a lot on stage recently and being more engaging with the audience in general. It felt awesome, and the gig went very well.

I have come to understand that I may need a refresher course every now and then. I should also put in some quality control checks on myself as well as make a conscious effort to be in the moment on a gig and really try to put forth a positive effort. In life, it can become easy to get complacent after doing the same thing over and over for a long time. I learn new songs, and I try to find new jokes to tell and new ways to interact with the audience. It is with good intentions that I start to think of how to make myself better, but it is with action that I find myself being the Solo Acoustic Musician that I want to be.

I have stayed true to my purpose of playing and singing music for the people in front of me. Some gigs go well for one set and then slip away during the next. I have come to understand that everything in life has its own yin/yang, good or bad, and that definitely includes gigs.

I have to stay vigilant and smile. In times of triumph on a gig, I feel very validated for my efforts, and in times of rejection or failure I feel ignored. It is a part of life and it is a part of the lifestyle I have chosen to live because I get on stage in front of a group of strangers every day and try my best. A constant in my life is the random audience. I really appreciate the crowds that clap and applaud my efforts and I really do hold nothing against the people on the nights when the audience is indifferent. I know I will be up there again tomorrow.

I am not preaching to you. I just want to help anyone I can to start or to become a better SAM than I am. I wish you all the best in your pursuit of playing and singing well. Also, I wish you well to earn a living while leaving a stamp on the world by providing happiness to any audience you are in front of. I believe we can all use our talents to enhance another person's life and make them smile. For an afternoon or an evening, for just an hour or two, a SAM can help them feel happiness. Get to it and don't ever stop! It is a calling and you can do it! You can make a difference in someone else's life with your music.

Don't sit on the bench; get in the game! Practice everything... playing your guitar, singing, booking, being on time, having a positive attitude... everything!

You can create your own personal lifestyle and make a living playing music as a Solo Acoustic Musician.

ABOUT THE AUTHOR

Michael Nichols has been a singer-songwriter and working musician for thirty years. He currently lives in the Tampa Bay area of Florida. Growing up singing in a church choir and in the school chorus was the beginning of his life in music. He tried several other instruments before putting his hands on a guitar, but didn't really get into the drums, piano, violin, or saxophone. He started gigging for money when he was fourteen years old and has played music in just about every situation possible. He is still playing almost three hundred gigs a year and staying busy in his community. As a Paul Harris Fellow involved with Rotary International, he has donated money and time into charitable activities over the years.

 **ACKNOWLEDGMENTS**

A very special thanks to my two biggest fans, my little sister and my nephew!

I love you both more than you know...

Thank you to Edward Porcelli for his support and inspirational text messages nudging me along to keep writing. Ed is a baseball coach and also the author of the book Scabs Heal All Wounds, a true story of a replacement player during the baseball strike in the '90s.

My deepest gratitude goes out to my great friend Donna for her support, encouragement, and her memory of lots of stories I have told her in the past.

Thank you to all the owners and managers who have hired me over the years. I appreciate being given the chance to live a life through my music.

Thank you for buying and reading this book. Go check out the website for SAM merch: soloacousticmusician.com

Printed in Great Britain
by Amazon